Loving Isadora

The Isadora J. Seibert Foundation

Printed in the United States of America

First Printing, 2017

ISBN 978-1-365-83517-9

http://www.isadoraseibert.org/

Preface

Born on May 27, 1988, my daughter, best friend, middle child,
soul mate, and role model left her human body on March 6, 2014
at the age of twenty-five.
Her name is Isadora Johanna Seibert.
Our immediate family consists of my husband, Richie, our son,
Hilton and daughter-in-law Traci, Dora (our affectionate nickname
for her), and our younger daughter, Tania.
Dora was also a granddaughter, niece, cousin, friend to all,
high school science teacher, tennis coach,
club advisor, optimist, volunteer, and shining light.

To read more about her, please visit isadoraseibert.org

~~~~~~~

This book is about the love and comfort Dora continues to share
even though she is no longer in her body. These experiences are
just a handful of the many ways she has made her presence known
as she continues to daily. Whatever your situation may be, this
book is meant to uplift your heart and to put your mind at ease. If
you were fortunate enough to have known her, you would easily
agree that Dora's presence in this life always did that for those
around her.

Chapter One
The Magic Begins

It is too difficult to share with you the hour that preceded the moment of Isadora's passing. It is enough for you to know that there could be no greater inner agony possible for two parents than losing a child and then being expected to continue living. I had not been separated from Isadora for more than three or four sleep hours per day since her diagnosis, and even during those hours, I was sleeping in the same room with her. My whole existence was Dora's well being at every moment. Suddenly, when she "left," I had no idea how Dora was, where she was, or even *if* she was. I cannot describe what occurred after her passing. I will just share that my post-traumatic stress keeps me from giving details.

A couple of hours afterward, I kept repeating that I just needed to know that she was okay; that she is still okay. I told myself that I could survive this horror if I knew that. Please, Dora, please give me a sign that you are okay. I never thought that I would survive life long after her passing, nor did I have the desire to. Truthfully, since she has passed, there have been times when I still haven't moved very far from this feeling. But, in those darkest moments of utter despair, I would have made any deal or said anything to get a response about my beloved Dora.

Richie, my husband, spoke calmly through his tears. "We just need to be patient. We have to keep our eyes open and wait for something to happen." Before Richie could finish saying the word "happen", the buzzer on the alarm clock next to my bed went off. This was my work clock, set to play classical music weekdays at 7:00 am. The alarm had not been set for five months. Not only was it now going off in the middle of the afternoon, it was making a buzzer sound and not playing music. We gasped. It had to have been Dora, sending us the message that she heard us, that she was okay, and that she was still here. This happened less than an hour after she left.

Within seconds of the alarm sounding, Richie's mom called. She said, "I just talked with your father and Isadora is with her grandfather." In 1962, Richie's father had passed at the age of 37 from pulmonary fibrosis. At that time, only 39 people in the world had come down with the disease. Richie could not speak. In a sad similarity, Dora had passed from a disease that only 200 people per year worldwide are first diagnosed with. Richie thanked his mom for the message and ended the call. We felt that the magic had begun.

Chapter Two
She Speaks

Dora's brother, Hilton, was desperate to receive a sign from her. It was now the following day and Richie and I had already felt Dora communicating with us. In the evening, Hilton and our daughter-in-law, Traci, returned to their home after spending the day with us. When Hilton and I hugged to say goodbye, he sadly whispered that he wanted and needed a personal sign from his sister. I remember whispering back to him "Ask her for one." When Hilton arrived back at his place, he sent me the following text:

I got my sign. I turned on my Apple TV and this was the screen I saw.

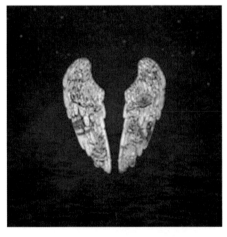

New Coldplay album. Wings for the album cover. First song is *Always in My Head.*

Dora knew that Hilton had always been a Coldplay fan. The timing, the image, and the song title were more than a coincidence for him. Hilton entered into the realm of signs from the afterlife with us.

Chapter Three
A New Friend Moves into Our Yard

Dora started communicating with us in new and creative ways after
the incident with the alarm clock and my son's television. One day,
while staring out the window into the backyard, we saw a cardinal
fly by. In the world of spiritual healing and the beyond, cardinals are
often associated with a loved one who has passed on. Since that
initial sighting, a number of cardinals have moved in to our yard.
They often sit and wait for us to see them and then they fly off. We
have even opened the front door of our house and found one
sitting there on the steps waiting to be acknowledged. It often

seems like they want to come inside the house. One flew directly at me from a tree top and stopped in midair about one foot away from my face. We feel these, and other birds, have been sent to us by Dora. Her message is always the same. I am still here. I am still with you. I love you still.

Chapter Four

Two Halves Make a Whole

It only hurts to think about the wedding Dora never got to plan, the son-in-law that we didn't see bring her joy, or her children that will not be coming forth for us to love. When her brother was getting married, Dora had imagined herself having a wedding in upstate New York on the property where our vacation home is. She pictured a huge tent on the lawn and everyone dancing and kids jumping in the pool. She envisioned it all natural and beautiful and filled with love. I can't say whether that vision would have ever taken place when she was ready to marry but I mention it because of something she said to me.

On one of the last few days of Dora's life, she was crying and through her tears she said, "It's okay, Mom, that I never got married. I married you. You were like my husband."

I can't say what it is that I provided for her, but she made *me* feel whole. We were able to finish each other's sentences, share our deepest secrets, love each other unconditionally, and be our happiest when together. We weren't even two halves making a whole. It was as if we were one person.

Chapter Five
Thirds Equals One Whole, Too

While Dora was a student at Ramapo College of New Jersey, she made many great friends and was very active in campus life. We, of course, were so happy for her and loved to hear about all of it. I clearly remember one evening when Richie and I each had a laptop in front of us and we were both simultaneously talking with Dora using AIM (one of the original forms of instant messaging.) We had different questions for her, typing different conversation topics, but we both held the same thirst for wanting to be connected to her. Dora thought it was so funny that her dad and I were inches apart from each other but were messaging her separately. She was having trouble keeping up with both "conversations" simultaneously but she loved how much she was being loved. Dora told me days later that she had felt so lucky being close to her parents as she had seen that not everyone had that experience. She never realized that it was *she* who made that exchange of love so easy and that it was *we* who were the lucky ones.

Chapter Six

Her 26th Birthday Party

The day *after* her passing, I was in my bedroom when I heard Dora say, in my mind, that she wanted a big birthday party with all of her friends invited. The anniversary of her birthday was still two months away but I was already dreading the agonizing sadness that it would bring. Dora must have known that and clearly sent me her wish in the hopes that it would help us through her birthday. I thought back to a Facebook post she dictated to me about a month before she passed. I would fulfill her wish to have a celebratory party and use the occasion of the anniversary of her birth to do it.

Isadora's Facebook Post

February 9, 2014

Dearest Friends and Family,

I wish to apologize for not responding to your texts and emails although I greatly appreciate them. For now, I am not feeling well enough to respond but I enjoy reading them. I understand that it is difficult to know what to say to me because even I don't know how to respond to what is happening (for those of you who don't know, cancer.) Please know that I do not expect anyone to message me in any form but if you choose to that is wonderful. Some days are better than others. Right now, I am going through a rough patch. Again, please forgive me for not responding to you. I love you all. I feel so appreciative of your friendship, love, and support. Thank you for every prayer, gift, and kind thought. When I am healthy again, I would like to show my gratitude by hosting a celebratory party. You are all invited. Thank you for staying friends with me through this terrible time. I love you with all my heart.

On May 27, 2014, which would have been Dora's 26th birthday, her closest friends were invited to our home for a "thank you for loving her" BBQ. Her birthday fell on a Tuesday, a work day. In the early evening, over 70 wonderful people gathered to show their support and share friendship. Some traveled hours. Some could only make it for the last hour. More wanted to come but couldn't make it. The concern for our family, the sympathy, and all the love was so very humbling to us. It was such a reflection of who Dora was and the kind of people who were in her life.

Chapter Seven

Phone Call with a Medium – April 2014

Our suffering was so great that there didn't seem to be a way out. I was searching for mediums online. I needed to know how my beautiful child was. I needed answers. I came across a woman who was certified by the Forever Family Foundation, a volunteer organization that raises awareness through scientific research and true mediumship about what happens to our souls after our bodies die. I found someone who lived a half hour from my home and emailed her right away. It would take, as noted on her website, up to ten days to receive an email reply regarding an appointment. Once I received her email response, the actual session might have to wait as long as two months. I felt that at least I set the ball in motion.

Richie came home just then with a phone number; he handed it to me and said that someone had given him the number. This person had lost her mother and, after a year, went to see this medium that was recommended to her by a friend. She found the experience to be very healing. I called the number to make an appointment and left a message of just our first names and phone number. Within 15 minutes, the phone rang. It was the medium returning our call. Prior to the call, I had been feeling a strong need to purchase a tree to plant in the yard in honor of Dora and I shared this with Richie. He readily agreed but felt that since it was a cold and rainy day, the purchase should wait for better weather. I had been hearing thoughts from Isadora since her passing. I knew it was Dora who requested the tree. Therefore, I felt the weather should not be an obstacle.

The medium had no information other than our first names. Richie put the call on speaker so that we both could hear and participate in the call. The medium, a very sincere and honest man named Bob Murray, asked how we got his number because he does not advertise. He explained that he charges $175 for however long the session lasts and that it could go on for 2 to 3 hours. Bob instructed us to write down questions that we had for the spirit, (our daughter unbeknownst to him), and if our questions weren't answered during our meeting, we could ask them at the end. We were not to tell him the questions beforehand.

After he shared this information, Bob said, "Wait. I have chills going up and down my back. The spirit is very present. I see its arms are open in a u-shape as if it is hugging you both." He said not to tell him anything, such as gender or our relationship to the spirit, as he wanted the meeting to be pure. We were instructed to answer any questions with a simple "yes" or "no" on the phone, if applicable. The following is a sampling of what came streaming from the medium over the phone. His words are first, our answers are in parentheses, and the information in italics has been added to increase your understanding:

~~~~~~~

Is this spirit one of three? (yes) *Isadora is one of three siblings and frequently did things alone with her parents, creating a threesome.*

Whose birthday is in May? The spirit is telling me she wants a big celebration on that day. *This was confirmation of what I heard Dora say to me about her upcoming birthday.*

Go plant a tree. The spirit wants a tree. *At the end of the call, we left to purchase Dora's tree to plant in the yard. The weather was no longer an issue for Richie!*

Richie needs to pay attention when driving – the spirit is telling me that he is very distracted when he is driving. The spirit wants Richie to drive carefully on his upcoming trip. *Dora did not enjoy being driven by her dad ! She felt he was very inattentive and inconsiderate to other drivers. She scolded him frequently. Two days after the call, Richie was to drive to Pennsylvania on a previously planned trip to see relatives. Clearly, Dora was worried.*

Set a place for this spirit at the table with your family this weekend because the spirit is saying it will definitely be there. *Dora was very family-minded and loved extended family gatherings. That upcoming weekend was the first gathering to take place since her passing. Richie drove more consciously. There was a place setting for Dora at the table of her aunt and uncle's house.*

We felt such a connection that we could not wait to meet with this medium in person. A few minutes after the call ended, the medium called back to say that the spirit is lingering with him. It was telling him that the spirit was like a mom to Richie, not his actual mom, but that their relationship was like a mother and son. Dora was nurturing like a mom to everyone but she was more like a corrective guide to her dad, instructing him to do the right thing. It was a very

14

accurate description of a small part of their relationship. We felt hopeful that the medium was to be the beginning of receiving answers to our questions and alleviating our tremendous pain.

Dora's Apple Tree
In celebration of her love, and a life so beautifully lived
1988 - 2014

Here is the apple tree and plaque when it was first planted, with rocks placed underneath (some painted) in the shape of hearts. Whenever we find a heart shaped rock somewhere out in nature, we place it there.

Chapter Eight
TV Talking

Visiting our vacation home for the first time without Dora was beyond difficult. Richie drove the two hours and I cried the entire drive. Every passing landmark reminded me of the many times I had driven with Dora to this very place, a joyful experience that we would never share again. Twenty five years of us taking the drive together, excited about the fun that was to come, was over. Richie and I couldn't even speak until we arrived. In the evening, I was lying down in our bedroom. Richie had been watching television in the living room. He got up to make some food in the kitchen. The TV, a fairly new 60 inch television, could be seen from the kitchen. All of a sudden, the TV turned off. Richie went to see what had caused this unexpected occurrence. It did not matter what he tried; Richie could not get the television to turn back on. Believe me, he tried it all. Why would such a thing happen? Since we had already had an experience of Dora trying to communicate with us through electronics, Richie felt that it was Dora saying hello. Since she was new to the afterlife, perhaps Dora did not have the communication thing completely mastered yet as she was not able to get the television back on either ! The television was finished. Though it turned out to be a very expensive hello, we appreciated it nonetheless and asked Dora to keep it up.

Chapter Nine
Something Else Happened There, Too

For at least 15 years prior, we had spent every Christmas through New Year's school break at our vacation home. I think Dora may have missed only one year and that was because she was celebrating in London on a trip with her very close friend Allie. New Year's Eve of 2014 turned out to be her last time at her beloved New York home. Members of our extended family joined us there. Everyone who could be there came. Dora was already ill but feeling well considering. She was so happy to be there with her family. A couple of weeks later in January, even more extended family (14 of us) would join her on a trip to Disneyworld. With the exception of her upstate house, Walt Disneyworld Resort in Florida was her favorite place. We had been to Disneyland in California and even Disneyland Paris together. But Disneyworld was her home away from home. Dora had vacationed there just about every year of her life. She was feeling so optimistic about the trip and her health that she generously, lovingly, and humorously had special shirts made for each family member that was going on the trip.

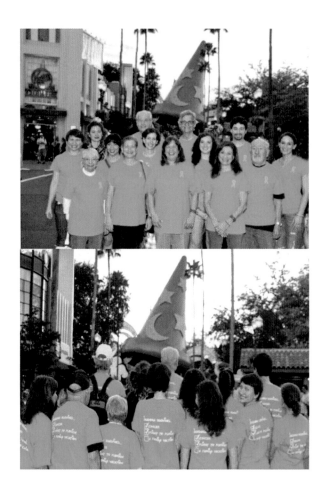

Very sadly, however, during that trip, Dora's health took a turn for the worse. She struggled and continued to struggle until she left us in March of that year.

Looking for comfort that first visit back to the house in April, I went into her room. It was devastating to look at her things. I did not find comfort, only agony. Then, tucked away, I saw something which Dora had curiously bought at an estate sale a couple of years prior. Neither she nor I knew exactly why she wanted this completed sand art picture but she did. It took my breath away when I saw it again. I understood now of the foreshadowing of her purchase. Finding this sand art design of hers brought Richie and I much comfort.

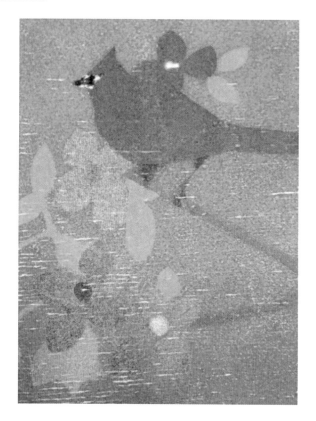

Chapter Ten

Transcript of Meeting with Medium Bob Murray

(the medium we had previously spoken with on the phone)

April 2014

*Our responses are in parenthesis.

Additional information to help with understanding is in italics.

I am getting that this has been a tumultuous time in both of your lives. (Yes.) Has this been going on for a period, I want to say, close to a year? (No.) It is a lesser time? (Yes.) But prior to a change, that is how I am going to word it, prior to a change in your lives, was there a tumultuous time leading up to this change? (Yes.) So the year makes sense now? (Well, it wasn't a year). In other words, there was a leading up to it. (Yes.) *We view the change as the passing of Isadora. The time between her diagnosis and her passing was approximately five months and they were most certainly tumultuous.*

The word that keeps coming up, it's repetitive "timing, timing, timing". In other words, the timing was not supposed to be. Does this make sense? (Yes.) Was it something to do with anything in the head region? (No.) Were there any kind of like headaches or something? (Oh, yes.) Did it turn into something more severe like migraines? (Yes.) Did this person become immobilized because of this pain? (Yes.) It's almost like a blackout. When you get a headache like this, it is so severe that you have to keep your eyes closed; the light, sounds, can just send you into a tizzy. I'm getting something and it is funny because over this I am getting "I'm okay,

I'm okay." *Dora had three very serious migraines in a ten day period that led us to the ER, where she was given a brain scan. Nothing abnormal was found. It was one week later to the day that we were in yet a different ER for abdominal symptoms. It was there that she had an abdominal cat scan and received her terminal diagnosis.*

This is a female? (Yes.) There's something, I don't even know how to put this in words to you, but it's coming, and it has nothing to do with you, but there is something about a neglect, something was neglected and it had nothing to do with you. Does this make sense? (Yes). And because of this neglect, somebody somehow dropped the ball. Time was of the essence and time escaped. (Yes.) *We have agonized over whether there was a way to have been more medically proactive and if, perhaps, Dora's cancer would have been found sooner. However, the horror of this cancer, fibrolamellar hepatocellular carcinoma, is that there are no routine tests that would raise a red flag. Symptoms usually only appear once it is too late. It is diagnosed with a cat scan but if there are no symptoms, there is no reason to have a cat scan prescribed. We do feel like we dropped the ball but we also know that there was no way to have seen this coming.*

There seems to be an onslaught in the last decade, I have seen it. I have heard it where people are leaving the planet. They are leaving. They are going back to their home. Biblically, or from whatever religion, there is always a basis "as on Earth so it is in Heaven". Everything is duplicated. By that, what I mean is their environment, what they liked the most. They will not come back to you in a dream as they were. They will come back to you how they were at their best. So let's say hypothetically, wait - who had the jackhammer? Who worked with a jackhammer? (I don't know). I see them doing this. (demonstrates using a jackhammer) Did you bowl? (Richie: A long time ago. Yes.) This person, this male is stepping in and saying hello. Saying hello. *We still have not figured out the jackhammer connection or why Richie was asked about bowling. He did take our three kids bowling occasionally, when they were young, while we were staying at our vacation house. Maybe Dora was about to talk about that when another spirit stepped in. Richie hoped it was his dad, who had passed when Richie was about nine years old. We don't know. We were too busy smiling at such an interruption to focus on this "intruder."*

You both have good energy. I have to tell you that. You really do. So, people are leaving and going back to the arms of God; they are going back to where they were created. In heaven, there is no time. Time is man-made. Let's say, hypothetically, that this woman has passed say five months ago, maybe three months ago. That could be three seconds in God's time. There are things that have been occurring that I think you have been missing because they are trying to get your attention to let you know that they are okay. *He demonstrates hugging himself.* I'm seeing an embrace, like a reassurance, to say to you that what's done is done. What is important for you to know is that she is walking briskly, she's not limping, she's not shuffling – she is walking briskly. Does this make sense? (Yes.) *For the last 12 hours of Isadora's life, she wasn't able to move her muscles on her own. It was very, very comforting that she was showing the medium that her body worked again.*

She is a very interesting soul. I see that there were talents that she did not utilize. She wasn't a braggart. What's this with the sister?

(She has a sister.) Is this sister over on the other side or is the sister still here? (Here.) Who is Catherine? (I don't know.) Did she live next to somebody named Catherine? There is something about a Catherine. (I don't know.) It will come. It will come. Has the sister on this side kind of gone into the abyss with this passing? (I am not sure.) Has she gone into like a bubble? She is feeling her own vulnerability at this point. That would be a given for anybody.

Was there a transference that had to do with a hospital? Was she supposed to go to another hospital? (She was at three different hospitals over five months for varying amounts of time.) Was St. Barnabas the last hospital? (Yes.) She wants you to get over the anger. Besides the grief, there is anger for you, Phyllis. (Yes, toward God.) I understand what you are saying but understand in the Law of God, does he make the rules? Yes. But, we have free will. We have free will. That is the gift that he gave us. You know, I have heard stories from parents losing their children, and they go "why?" And they turn against religion and it is unfortunate. *At this point in the session, the medium did not know that we had lost a child and that she was the reason we were meeting with him.*

Let me try to put this in perspective for you. It's going to take time but it will register for you. We come back many lifetimes. You have a zodiac sign. In that sign, there are positive elements and elements that need be worked on. There are twelve signs in the zodiac. Think about that. How many years do you go to school, minus college? Twelve. Each sign you come back and you're learning a different aspect. You choose the parent you have to come into this world.

You choose the experience. You came in to choose that lesson. You choose the family and the rest happens. We are here to learn lessons. This is school. This is a temporary reprieve. We are given that grace. What is holding the soul back, and what could hold you back, is when you hate something, or you are angry with something, the only one that it is going to affect is you. I am not judging you. On the spiritual path that you are on, you need to allow that soul to flourish and they don't want you to be bitter. They don't want you to go into a tailspin. They understand the grieving process. They get all that. But, they don't want you to not lead your life because now you are wasting valuable time. They have already moved on. What we, as humans, miss is the ability to pick up the phone, and know that they are there. We miss the fact that we can get in a car and go from point A to point B and we know they are there. We miss the fact that we can take them shopping and this, that, or whatever. We are selfish as human beings.

Energy does not die. You need to understand something that you've been feeling for a while (*he is looking at Richie*) that in your goodness, in your kindness, and you are kind of like a gentle giant, that you feel like you have been taken advantage of. Just yes or no? (Yes.) You need to understand that you are being blessed. It has not been forgotten and overlooked. The people who did what they did, that is their karma. Whatever they have done, that is their issue. That's the lessons they need to learn. You stay steadfast because there is going to be a turnaround for you. You mark my words. You keep your head up. Don't change. Use discernment. Don't be so willing to open your wallet. Use discernment and help those that you feel are worthy. The rest of them, "no" is the answer. Don't let them drain you because they have drained you. Does that make sense what I am saying? (Yes.) You hold steadfast because things are turning around for you. You are not over-the-hill. It is not the end of the road. There are new beginnings that are coming up for you. New beginnings. Hang in there. Spring is renewal. Don't become sedentary. Get out. Get air. Get yourself to what you enjoy doing. It may not cost you anything. I don't care if you have to walk through the woods. Do what you need to do. She (*looks at Phyllis*) is not going to do it for you. She can't. You have to do it for you. Your partnership is a spiritual journey. It is not about the sex. It is not about the money. It is not about the house. It is not about the stuff. It is a spiritual journey that the both of you are taking. That's the commitment that you are in. I can see it. You've both been through the thick and thin of it. You've been through the war. You've been through the bullets. Ducking here and ducking there. But, you are survivors and you will continue to be because God has a plan for you. God has a plan for you. Don't give up hope. You can question. That's the human thing.

There is a story where a woman is on her roof because there is flooding. She asks God to help her. A rescue helicopter flies overhead and she waves it away. She says she is waiting for God's help. A lifeboat comes by and she waves it away. She says she is waiting for God's help. She cries out to God, asking why He hasn't come to help her. God replies, "Who do you think sent the helicopter and the lifeboat?" What's in front of us, we don't see.

What's the significance of a lily? I mean lily is Easter but what is the significance of a lily? (Not sure.) Make any sense to you? I am seeing lilies. They are a beautiful flower. They are spiritual. They come in beautiful colors. I am seeing white. *We are still not sure what the reference was here; although, a white lily bouquet was delivered to our home after Dora passed. Perhaps Dora wanted to share something with us about the friend who sent it. Later, we felt the significance of the lily had to do with a special person, not a plant. Lily was born a couple of months after Dora's passing. She is the beautiful granddaughter of a dear co-worker of Dora's. Lily's mom, Denyse, came to our home while she was far along in her pregnancy and gave Dora a professional massage to ease any distress. Denyse did not know that she was having a girl nor did she even decide on her name until after her birth. We feel that Dora was telling us that she was with Lily before she was born into this world, caring for her as Lily's mom had cared for Dora. Denyse has since opened Alchemy Mind and Body Wellness Day Spa in Princeton, NJ.*

I am going to make a suggestion for you, Phyllis. You need to write a letter. Sit down and write your thoughts on paper. Go outside. Go to the woods. Find a place to sit and read the letter to yourself after you write it. Read it. Put your feelings on paper and read it because you are internalizing. You are internalizing, internalizing, internalizing.

What's teaching? (I'm a teacher. My son is a teacher. My daughter is a teacher. The deceased was a teacher.) Are you still teaching? (I took time off.) I am hearing "teach, teach, teach." That's wonderful. God bless. In her methodology of teaching, there was a unique style. Makes sense? (Yes.) Kind of like took the lesson plans and followed protocol but went by her own style. *Dora loved teaching and creating interesting, student-centered lessons. She was loved by her students because of her unique and caring style.*

 What's this about a door that is half open? Is there a problem with a door? (I don't know.) Is it a squeak or is it something that just doesn't seem to want to close or you have to lift it by hand? I'm being told "fix the door." It's driving her nuts. Funny. "It is disturbing," she says. In a comical way. She is a funny woman. Strange sense of humor but funny. She is kind of the straight man in a team of comedians. There is humor there. (Richie: A very funny person, yeah.) *We are still unsure about the door reference. Sorry, Dora!* Was she reading a book that you have access to or you own? You have it in your possession? (Phyllis: I am reading all the books in her room now as a distraction.) You have not finished reading a book or have not touched it? I am being told to tell you "You need to read that book." I have no idea what it is about but she wants you to read that book. *The book of hers that I was reading at the time, Magicians by Lev Grossman, has a paragraph in it that I reached about two days later. It states as follows: "If there's a single lesson that life teaches us, it's that wishing doesn't make it so. Words and thoughts don't change anything. Language and reality are kept strictly apart – reality is tough, unyielding stuff, and it doesn't care what you think or feel or say about it. Or it shouldn't. You deal with it, and you get on with your life." This rang very true in relation to our new reality. It certainly felt like the last sentence was Dora speaking to my grief.*

Was she, I'm going to ask this to your husband, was she spiritually enlightened? Because that is what keeps coming up. (Yes.) I mean she was up there in the game. Spiritually enlightened. There were a lot of things that she questioned and a lot of things that she didn't buy into and that is the right thing to do. She was very skeptical. Well, she was more inquisitive and analytical and there is nothing wrong with it. It can drive you nuts but she kind of like dissected. It had to feel right for her. This is not me talking. It had to be right or step away. Do you follow? (Yes.)

What I am hearing is that there needs to be a gathering of the clan. What she wants is joy. It's like the north and the south. One group is thinking one way and another group is thinking another way and she is saying "Enough of this. This is stupid." She wants it to come all together. She says "Life is very precious. Life is very short. I am a perfect example of it. They need to stop this nonsense. They are wasting time." Bring it together and be done with it. You are being more selective of who you want to be around. You don't want to be around the negative. *This we did not understand at all because our extended family unit is very close. It was only when we went out to lunch with two of her very close friends, Marlene and Christine, whom she met at college, did we know that this message was meant for them and all of her friends from Ramapo College. Dora often organized pot-luck dinners and hang outs with everyone. For the most part, these wonderful, loving, friends now physically live in either northern or southern New Jersey. After sharing this message, Marlene and Christine said they would work on keeping all of the friendships together, as Dora would have done.*

There was a postponement of something to do with a trip. Does this make sense to the both of you? (Yes.) Okay. I am being told to tell you that you need to go on this trip. Was this on a boat? Were you going on a cruise? (No, but a boat was involved.) But you were going away? (Yes.) I am being told to tell you "What are you waiting for?" Leave a sign on the door "gone fishing," whatever, and do it. You need to step out of the box. *Our immediate family, including Dora, had reservations to visit the new addition to the World of Harry Potter at Universal Studios in Orlando during the September Jewish holiday school closings (4 out of the 6 of us were teachers then, now 5 out of 6!). Our family consists of huge Harry Potter fans. It was a wishful-thinking carrot that we dangled before Dora, knowing that the odds were slim that she would be able to make it. We planned to stay at a hotel on the property that transports guests to the park by ferry boat. We canceled the trip once we saw things turning for the worst. We eventually took the trip 10 months after Dora's passing, in her honor. It was difficult as we felt her absence more than her presence. Even though her message was for us to go, and we honored that, it was too soon. We brought too much grief with us on that trip.*

Your environment, you've pulled the energy down. You've pulled it down. What happens, we as energy, we cloud things. You know they say you are what you eat. They say tell me who you hang around with and I will tell you who you are. You want to clear up the energy in your environment. Change the vibration level because in your innocence Phyllis, in your grieving process, you've brought that energy and you've clouded the area.

Was this your mom that crossed over? (No.) Was it a................this is a woman, yes? (Yes.) Not old? (No.) I'm hearing "I'm not old. I'm not old." Bare with me, okay? (Yes.) Why do I keep getting 34? (I don't know.) Was she older than 34? (No.) She was younger than 34? Whoa, whoa. What the heck is 34? Was this person going to go back and continue something? A degree? (Yes.) Was this not a Masters but a Ph.D? (No, it was a Masters.) Okay. Slow down, slow down. *Medium talking to Dora.* She is reminding me that I said something about a mother to you and she said "I was a mother to everybody." She chose to be that. She was wide open. She was wide open. She is telling me "Thank you for getting that right." You're welcome. Oh boy. She put me in my place. Yeah, she was nurturing. *Dora was an extremely nurturing person. She cared for everyone with equal kindness, attention, and love.*

She is telling me that things are still as they were. Does this have something to do with your environment? (Yes.) Nothing has been touched. Nothing has been altered. "Things are still the same," she is telling me. She is saying, "Thank you." She is saying, "Thank you." My God. She is telling me a lot. I'm just trying to slow her down. She is like this. *Snaps fingers three times quickly.* She is trying to show me a lot of stuff and I'm trying to get her to calm down. *Her possessions have not been disrupted in anyway.*

I am getting a hair color. I want to say auburn. Were there reddish tints in her hair? Was there a kind of curl? Spit curls? (Yes.) Pretty. A model. Could have, should have, would have. I hear you. I'm talking to her. Aspirations, do you know what I am saying? (Yes.) Makes sense? (Yes. She was tall.) *She did attend an audition for fun in NYC a few years ago to be a contestant on America's Next Top Model show. She would have been pleased to have been chosen, but she was not. Years later, a student from the high school where she taught was selected for the show. She loved watching and rooting for her.*

Was her diet not so… because she was busy, busy, busy busy, busy…..was her diet not so good? (Yes, that's correct.) I am hearing her say "Shame on me." She's telling me that she placed herself more for others than for herself. She was that kind of, her stuff was secondary as opposed to whomever. Once again, she is saying "lessons, lessons." *Sometimes she would skip lunch or eat very little while at work because of how busy she was. However, Dora was a vegetarian from birth and remained so throughout her life. She was more respectful than most about eating healthy.*

What's this with the balloon? She is holding a balloon. A big balloon. It doesn't have any writing on it but I am seeing a balloon. And I'm seeing the color purple. *We did not know what this referred to and thought perhaps it had to do with the party she had asked us to host for her friends on her birthday. We were later told by a very close friend and co-worker of hers that the high school where she taught had purple balloons in the hallways to raise awareness for the upcoming Relay for Life cancer fundraiser that would be held in town. Dora, ironically, had always volunteered for cancer fundraising events.*

Stay with me because this is tough for me to say. It is for the both of you. She's kind of strutting her stuff right now. She was the pride and joy. That is what I am hearing. Was this a child that passed? (Yes.) Your child? (Yes.) My condolences to the both of you. Hold my hand. The gentleness, she is saying that to you Rich, as the male figure, you were stern but fair because you only wanted the best for her. She understands that. She gets that.

They have a life review when they go to the other side, by the way. Everything that they've gone through, it's not to judge them but to show them. As driven as she was, and doing what she did, the time was just like running away from her and at this fever pitch that I'm getting. It was like not being able to see the other side, the other side of the tracks where it was almost like she was doing it but there was, I don't want to say hesitancy, but like she was not grasping for it, which is understandable. In a sense, there wasn't enough time to get at everything she wanted to get at. She didn't understand that. Now she understands.

What she is telling me is that she comes more than you think because that is also aiding in her soul. It is aiding in her soul. Does she want to hear the grief and the sorrow? No, she doesn't because she is in the presence of God. She is at home. There is no pain. There is only love. Everything is popped. Colors, everything. She is saying it is beautiful and music, music, music. Did she surround herself with music? (Yes.) Because she is surrounding herself with music. She is incorporating. I don't know what grade she taught, don't tell me, but did she work with young people in her teaching? (No.) (Richie: Well, she did when she taught religious school). She is embracing and she has kids all around her. She has her hands out and the kids are around her; kids that are on the other side. She's kind of like the Mother Teresa. She is like the care keeper of these kids and they are circling around her. Now, she is not with them all the time but it's almost like playtime with them and she is coordinating it. Doing this and doing that. She is like, "Yeah, jack of all trades – master of none."

Give me a minute. It's almost like she is talking to you but she is talking through me. So I am trying to word it as she is telling me. I don't want to make it sound like she is telling me to tell you. It is like she is talking through me as if she is talking to the both of you. You are going to come out of here more lighthearted and maintain the lightheartedness with you. That's what she is saying. *This meeting with the medium did lighten our very heavy hearts as we were filled with pain. It was replaced, for the most part, with gratitude that we had 25 love-filled years with Dora.*

She is saying "I might be gone physically but I'm not going anywhere spiritually." She is around and she wants you to pay attention. She wants you to know that you are getting the signs. She says did you get proof enough when you walked in? Did she get your attention? (In the first few minutes, Richie's phone – which he had silenced – started speaking out travel directions!) They learn how to do that. She is learning, she is telling me. *Electric chimes in room started to play.* I turned that off! I turned that off! Okay…They learn how to manipulate energy. The room, in an environment, will become the portal. It will be colder than the rest of the house. They will take the energy from that environment, that room, to raise their level, their vibration level, to ours because we vibrate at a higher level. You may see what is called an orb, which is a white light. Just pay attention. Pay attention to that.

She is pointing to you, Richie. She says you have a problem with your leg. There was no problem with your leg? (No.) Was there something about being uncomfortable with a shoe that you have dealt with? (Yes.) She says to me something about the arch with

your foot. She is saying "orthotics." Is it your left foot? (Yes.) *Richie*
had an appointment to have orthotics made for his arches when Dora was
diagnosed. He canceled the appointment.

When she was growing up, she says to me that you were like an
explorer, (*to Richie*.) Did you take her exploring? (Phyllis to Richie:
Yes, in the woods upstate at our house.) She is showing me that she
is picking up rocks and turning them over. You are explaining
things to her. She says that she was a little girl but you didn't treat
her like a pansy. I don't want to say tomboy, but you gave her that
edge and she acknowledged that. She is saying "thank you." She is
showing me a panoramic view of everything she did. Going up a
hill. Getting dirty. Turning over rocks. Pretty interesting.

She said that you, Phyllis, and she understands, but she says that
you were a worry-wart. Does that make sense, growing up? (Yes.)
She says that was an endearing quality. She says it became
unnerving because it was even in the adulthood of her young life.
Moms are moms. You never stop being a mom.

In her personal life, had she thoughts about wanting to settle down
or was she hesitant about what she was seeing all around her?
Because I am seeing both sides of the coin. As far as meeting
someone or dating, it's almost like, I don't want to say it didn't exist
for her but it was like there were too many other things that she was
doing. Does that make sense? (Yes.) Don't get me wrong. It wasn't
that she was disinterested. It wasn't prioritized. It wasn't a necessity.
The accessibility, the timing, and you have to have time. I'm not
seeing there was a commitment there because it was like that's not

important, this is important. What she was doing was important as opposed to that. Does that make sense to you? (Yes.)

People would go to her and I see buckets of "woe is me" that they were dropping on her feet. She was the counselor for people. She was the counselor. It never stopped. It did wear her down. I mean she may not have looked it but it did take a toll on her. Constantly being bombarded with stuff. They would spend half an hour talking about themselves and then ask "how are you?" By that time, what difference did it make? This is what I am getting. *Dora gave of herself wholeheartedly to others and she had a tremendously large and wonderful group of friends.*

What is this about pink? Did she wear a lot of pink? (Not as an adult but very often as a child.) Well, pink to me is the significance of love. That's the highest color for love. Pink. I am getting a lot of pink. She is probably sending that to the both of you.

She is telling me "Have Dad check the car." Are you having some issues with your car? Are you hearing something? You know your car better than anybody else. (No, got some lights on.) Check engine? Check it before you go on a trip. She is funny. She says sometimes you have to tell him twice. Am I right? He takes it in. He digests it. In his goodness, he will be complacent about it.

There is something that she is saying in a very gentle way, in a very loving way. She is encouraging the both of you, when you are ready, to put your heads together and write. She wants you to write a memoir that will help other families that are going through what you have gone through. She said the both of you collaborating together will be of help to others. It will be of assistance to others.

You could not do it if I were still here. She wants to encourage you to do that. I am being shown a butterfly. She wants it on the book. Up on the right hand corner. However you title it, that's your decision. But it has to come from the both of you, no third party. Gather your information. She says I will help you write it. I will be your instrument. But, you need to ask. Don't expect me to just show up. But I will guide you. You have to invite her in. There is a protocol and you have to invite her in. There is free will and she is not going to invade that. She is going to assist you. She is encouraging you to do this. She is giving you the inspiration. It can be poignant and humorous at the same time. Someone is going to connect with it. Assist those to heal.

She is showing me a ribbon, Phyllis, and she is tying it. Does this make sense to you? (Yes. It's an image I used to teach writing lessons when I taught third grade.) Do the book together. *You are now reading the book Dora asked us to write to help others.*

She wants you to take better care of yourself. She says you are like the Ever Ready bunny and you need to change the batteries every once in a while. There is no pampering going on with you, Phyllis. She wants you to pamper yourself. She says you have to. You have to do it.

She is a good kid. She is a good kid. In growing up, what she is showing me – and you said she was the middle child (Yes.) – she is indicating to me that she never felt like she was stuck in the middle, like as described in the birth order book. It was equal. She is grateful for that. She acknowledges that. And she says that is all about love. She thanks you for that.

36

The oldest is the son? She is the middle, correct? She was in the wedding party? (Yes.)Was there some kind of discrepancy of flowers at the wedding? (I don't think so.) She is pointing out something about flowers. What is this about engineering? She is pointing to her brother. Did he want to go to engineering school? (No.) Why am I getting engineering? Both hands and head, the son. Not just the head. This (*points to hands*) has to work with this (*points to brain.*) I am seeing they are incorporated. He will do well. *Dora's brother is a high school math teacher. He also has a computer business where he creates programs, commercial websites, and does installations and repairs. He used to help manage the high school's chess club but is now the school's robotics team advisor, and is the boys' tennis coach at the school and go-to tech person. He is presently working on his Masters Degree, as well. Perhaps the engineering has to do with the robotics club — which at the time with the medium, he had not begun yet.*

Now the youngest, still in school? (She is getting her Masters in Teaching.) What I am getting here, Phyllis and Rich, is that she is pursuing something, or doing something, in retrospect to her sister who has passed. She wants to do something as a fulfillment both for herself and in honor of her sister. I don't know if it is the pursuing of education but I want to say that it goes beyond that. Does this make sense? (Richie: Time will tell.) I am seeing it internalized right now. There is a determination. The best thing I can say to your children is to tell them to be open. Pay attention to their surroundings. That is how spirit will get their attention. They can turn a radio on. They can turn the TV on. They can manipulate lights. They can do a lot of stuff to get your attention. They will get your attention. (Dora has many times! *Tania, our youngest, has since earned her Masters and teaches high school English courses. She is also the editor of this book!*)

Were there some issues going on with the digestion or the stomach? (Yes.) I don't know if it had something to do with her intestines or her private area. I am getting an overlap. Was there a lot of vomiting? (Yes.) She was mad. (Yes, she was.) She was mad. She was having trouble processing it all. (Yes.) At first, it was like minor – it will go away but then it intensified. It knocked her for a loop she says.

Go ahead and read the questions you brought.

(Phyllis: Does she know why she was taken at such a young age?) There are things that she has to do on that side that need to be addressed. There is a shortness of time, as she is putting it to me, for all of us on this planet. I am not saying doom or gloom but they see things differently. To some degree, there is a level of protection that she was given, as bizarre as that sounds to you. There are things coming within the social structure that are changing, that are going to change. She is helping those that are coming. She is part of the committee, part of the masses of the welcoming committee. She is an organizer. She is helping. She is helping. She is learning, too. It is all new.

(Phyllis: Are we going to see each other again?) Yes, she is going to come and visit you both in a dream. She is going to reassure you that everything is okay. Yes, and when, in God's time, it is your time to go back home, she is going to be the first one at the gate. She said you won't need E-ZPass. She is so funny.

(Phyllis: Did she meet any relatives?)

Two women.

(Which side?) Both sides of your families. Two men or three? Three men.

(Richie: They are with her?)

They were part of the entourage that was there when she crossed over. The welcoming committee.

(Richie: Was it my father?)

I am being shown on your side, two men. (Phyllis: She didn't know them.) It doesn't matter. It doesn't matter. They knew her. Your father, was he about your stature, Rich? (yes) Because I see a man bending down to her. He is kind of like bending down. Was she about 5'5? (taller). He is bending down to her. (He was 6'4). 'They are showing me the ropes,'" she says.

(Phyllis: Did she know that she was going to take her last breath when she did?)

It was almost like…

(Phyllis: because for me it was a shock – she was going to take a nap and I was fixing her pillows. I asked her "Is that better?" She said, "Yes" and then she just instantly passed.)

It was almost like she was having visions. Someone was in the room with her, a spirit. Someone was there with her to help her make that transition, being with her at that moment. You hear stories about the angel of death. I am not getting that. Someone was with her that she recognized as being there to help her crossover and get her into the light. Sometimes when people are not ready to go, they get stuck. She went. (snaps finger). She was gone.

(Richie: What's 605?)

I want to say it could be the time of her passing, or a room number. I want to say it's a room number.

(One day, she said to me '605. Dad, it's 605.' I asked her what she meant and she just said "605." It wasn't that time when she said it.) Here, look up the number in this book. Angel Numbers: the meaning of number sequences. Go ahead and read what 605 means. Richie: "God is helping you to improve your life so that you can have more peace of mind." (Richie: cool book). There it is. That is 605. *A week later, we did some research on the number 605 and what we found is shared further in this chapter. A couple of months after that, we felt the final clarification of what Dora was telling us with the number 605. This, too, will be explained to you.*

(Richie: Is there anything she wanted to tell me because she went so fast and unexpectedly. I wasn't in the room. She passed on March 6th. She was diagnosed on October 19th.)

Wow! So recently! Was it cancer?

(Yes. She died of a very rare cancer, fibrolamellar hepatocellular carcinoma. Only 200 new cases a year worldwide. Only 60 in the U.S. It mostly strikes young, healthy people usually in their teens or 20's. Not enough people live long enough for them to figure it out. She was first diagnosed at Overlook Hospital. From there, we went by ambulance to Memorial Sloan-Kettering. After about ten days, we decided to take her home. Later on, we went to St. Barnabas whenever we needed help. We contacted a psychic healer who eased her pain after leaving Memorial Sloan-Kettering. She didn't need any medication after her first meeting with him. He took care of her.)

(Phyllis: We had a family meeting and we talked about what we each wanted when we passed. Dora said she wanted to be cremated and buried at our vacation property. So a few days after she passed, we had a memorial service. Many, many people came. She positively affected so many people in her life. We did not, however, bury her remains.)

That's just the tip of the iceberg because more wanted to come but couldn't make it for whatever reason. More would have been there. You would have had a mob scene. I will tell you, and what she is telling me, is that it has changed a lot of lives. Throughout all ages, not just you and your husband and your immediate family. But throughout, it has changed a lot of lives. People are re-thinking about what they have been doing in their lives. They are re-tooling. In her uniqueness, she is telling me, that is one way to get the message across. Talk about getting attention. Bring it to attention. Sometimes you have to make the sacrifice to get something jump started. She was like the sacrificial lamb. They may come up with a cure and she may be the name on it.

(Phyllis: She did sign a paper to donate some of her tissue when they did a biopsy so it could be studied to try to find a cure. Richie: We started a foundation, too.)

Well, from your lips to God's ears that it does come to fruition; that these other 199 families will have their families stay intact because of the sacrifice that your daughter made. One could only hope and pray.

(Phyllis: Ironically, she was a very big volunteer and of all the things that she volunteered for, the most for were events that had to do with cancer and then she got cancer.)

It makes you wonder why of all the things for her to do, she chose those things. It was no coincidence. She did because that is who she is. That is her drive. I will be honest with you, you don't hear that about young people these days. A lot of kids have their own agenda. She was driven. I hope that for the both of you, you come to a point, that you both realize, that you did the best you could as parents and went above and beyond. You had those 25 years with her. (Phyllis: we are grateful) You had at least that. And 25 goes like that. (*Snaps fingers.*) You had that. I can't put myself in your place but my heart is with you.

I don't take to everybody. I can't or I'd go nuts but I will always be there for you and I say that to you with love. We all come from the same light. Your daughter would want me to do that. I was never a parent so I can't wrap my head around it. I can't fathom it. I don't have all the answers to life. I am thankful to God for what he has given to me. Spirits tell me what they want me to hear and that's it and then they cut me off. They know that they need to do what they need to do. Your daughter is going to communicate with you on a different level. That's your child. I'm not your child. I'm just the messenger. But it will be more significant. When the timing is right, it will be more significant. You've gotten your signs and God bless that she is able to do it so soon and it will continue.

(Phyllis: A question that came up in this conversation. Within hours after she passed, we were in our room and sobbing. I said if I just knew that she was okay, then I would be okay. Just give me a sign.)

(Richie: I said let's pay attention. Then the alarm clock went off. It hadn't been set since Phyllis was still working back in October. And, it was always set to go off with music but it went off with a whirring sound. And then, ten seconds after that, my cell phone rang and it was my mom. She said that she talks to my deceased father all the time and that he said she is okay. She is with him.)

So, you got confirmation that he was there greeting her? Einstein's Theory of Relativity. Everything happens simultaneously just in different dimensions. The older you get, humans lose their ability to have that clarity.

(Richie: We are spiritual people, Phyllis and I. We understand, more than the average bear, how it all works).

She keeps tapping me on the head. She is doing this. (*Taps his own head.*)

(Phyllis: Maybe she has more to say, Richie. Sshhh!)

God bless. I can't tell you how you have enhanced my life today. It is rare. There are some that walk the walk, some talk the talk. Some walk, talk, and do. You are an example of walk, talk, and do. I have seen it all. It is rare when you can find someone that you can sit and have a congenial conversation with who doesn't make you feel like you are losing your mind when you talk about this stuff. Energy does not die. I can shut the lights off but there will still be electricity running through the wires. You don't see it.

(Richie's phone makes a sound.) Was that your phone?

(Phyllis: Dora was just confirming what you said.)

(Phyllis: Yesterday, Richie was in the kitchen cooking something and the TV was on in the living room. I don't know if Richie was thinking about her or what. It is a fairly new TV, maybe a year or two, and it just died. It just went off. Permanently.)

(Richie: It lost its ability to turn back on.)

She is still learning how to work with the energy.

(Phyllis: That's what I said! She is learning how to do this!)

Tell her don't touch the TV!

(Richie: I already took it to the dumpster.)

(Phyllis: She can get in touch with us anyway she wants. I hear her. I hope it isn't my imagination.)

What are you hearing?

(Phyllis: I hear her, not her voice, but I hear her in my head. I hear her telling me things that I wouldn't have thought of. So, I know it's not my thoughts. I hear her say "Please go into this drawer and give this bracelet to this friend. They will know what it means." Things like that.)

That is what they call telecommunication. Sometimes you think you are losing your mind.

(Phyllis: But I don't want it to be my imagination or wishful thinking.)

No, it's not. When you are resting, and your thoughts are clear, that's telecommunication. To answer your question, she is communicating to you via your mind. They can do it in a soft whisper. That's how spirit is. You are not hallucinating. Let it keep doing it.

(Phyllis: When she passed, I started screaming and I feel badly about that because I felt that she was sort of hovering, as if she was in the house for a couple of hours before she left. And I was screaming and I feel so badly if she heard that. I wish I had understood that she was going so that I could have just lovingly said, "It's okay. I love you." Instead, I was screaming "Don't go!" Then, I went to my room and fell to the floor screaming I'm so sorry for what seemed like forever. I couldn't save her and I just apologized over and over again.)

I respect what you are saying and I admire your strength and your honesty, Phyllis. What parent in their right mind would want to let their child go? You weren't prepared for it. Do not, under any circumstances, have any remorse about your screaming. That is a normal reaction. That is nothing to be ashamed of. And, if indeed, that was the case that you felt, and I am not personally getting it, that she was hovering that is because of her love for you and her father.

(Phyllis: Well, the day before she left she was crying and said, "I don't know what to do." I told her, "You don't have to do anything." She cried, "I feel like I need to go. My body isn't working anymore but I don't want to leave you.")

She hasn't left. The vehicle left. Picture yourself driving a car. You get out of the car. The car is there. You're here. Her vehicle is here. Her spirit is still living. Her spirit does not die. The vehicle is no longer working. The vehicle, this (*points to his body*) is for identification purposes only.

(Richie: So how long does a spirit stay in spirit form before it goes back into a vehicle?)

Good question. Keep in mind there is no time in heaven. What we equate as 100 years could be ten days in their time. I am just giving you a hypothetical. There is no time in heaven.

(Phyllis: But if we come again then how can we still be a spirit with the people who love us if we are busy living another life?)

(Richie: How long does the spirit stay?)

That's a very interesting question, Rich. I don't even know how to answer that because it is up to, in God's time, if that spirit is ready to say ...Okay, I want to go back. Let's just say that your son and your daughter-in-law have a child. How do you know whether your daughter decided to come back in that vehicle to be back in the groove again? I don't know how to answer that other than it is God's time. It is up to the soul and if the soul is ready to make that transition. You hear stories about people who have had near death experiences and they don't want to come back. Once they have a taste of it, they don't want to go back and it's like "Oh no. You're going back because there is stuff you still have to do." And poof! They are gone.

(Richie: Who says you are going back?)

(Phyllis: God, I guess.)

There is this white being. They never see God but they see this presence, this light. This loving light. They never see the face of God. They see this ever-present light and it is brilliant and this energy tells them, "You are going back."

(Phyllis: She was so evolved for her age.)

Probably an old soul.

(Richie: She was an old soul.)

(Phyllis: She is probably not coming back. She knew how to be a good person. She learned all the lessons. When you were talking about disciplining your child, we never had a problem. She was unbelievable.)

(Richie: Okay, you said she changed people's lives. So we had this memorial service and you can't believe how many people came. Anyway, two of her friends spoke. Her uncle spoke. Afterwards, there was a room where we went and people waited two and half hours on line to come and see us to pay their condolences. Two and half hours! I saw women come up with their kids. They said "She has changed the way I will live my life now. I just want to be kind because she was the kindest person ever.")

So you were given confirmation of what the impact is of what she did. The sacrifice that she made of giving her life.

(Phyllis: Well, was it her choice? No. You even said she was mad. She was mad.)

She had every right to be. She had every right to be.

(Phyllis: She said she got this disease two years too soon because she felt there is going to be a treatment. Why couldn't she have gotten it later? She didn't want to leave.)

Because whatever had to be placed in action had to be placed in action immediately. Those lives needed to change. So many people have changed now. Their lives would have gone down a different path and there would have been more loss. Think of the impact of the lives that she has saved and is saving as we speak.

You have to honor your grief but the key is to try and be busy but be busy together. Men are, by nature, stoic. They take a lot but we are just as emotional as anyone. It is our ingrained upbringing. We weren't taught to show emotion. Be who you are. If you need to vent, you do it. And don't be ashamed of it. But, don't let it hold you down. Rest assured. Your daughter will come to you.

Were you very methodical with ironing? (Phyllis: No.) Who was methodical with ironing? She showed me something with an iron. She thought it was kind of funny. (Phyllis: She was very particular about how she dressed everyday to go to teach. She dressed beautifully.) Did she use an iron? (Phyllis: Yes.) Okay. I'm seeing this iron but she is showing it to me in a comedic way. You know how you take your time when you iron. What I am seeing is whoosh, whoosh, whoosh! (Richie: That's probably true because she was always in a rush.)

On a health note for you, Richie. Have you been experiencing any pain here?

(Points to chest.) Nothing stress-wise or anything like that. When was the last time you had a physical?

(Richie: I go to the doctor every three months. Check my blood.) Okay, it's nothing bad. Just as a precaution because of what you have been dealing with emotionally. I am being shown to have it checked out just to be on the safe side. I place emphasis that it is a precautionary thing but she is advising me to tell you. Anything else?

(Phyllis: Does she know how much we love her?)

Absolutely. Absolutely, Phyllis. That is a given. That is a given. That is a given. It's almost like she says you breathe it, you sleep it, you eat it. That is a given. You are all connected at the cellular level, not just at the spiritual level. There is a part of you, a part of Rich, a part of her. Imagine you are standing indoors looking out through a window, and you see somebody shivering in the cold. You are inside and it is 70 degrees in your environment. You can feel for this person outside but you can't comprehend what they are feeling. She is surrounded in love. No pain. No stress. No worry.

(Phyllis: No sadness?)

No, no, no, no, no. Everything is pure love. Everything is innocence. It's a new experience of taking it all in. She's home. She's home. She's left school. We are still in school. She is home. She doesn't want the sorrow for the both of you to linger. It is new and it is understandable. In a year from now, you are still going to have the memory but you want to be in a better place. You don't want to get ill from this. It won't do your kids any good. It won't do your family members any good. There are stories where people just give up. They lose the will to live.

(Phyllis: I was seriously suicidal for a couple of weeks afterward.)

Listen, God bless your brutal honesty. But, I want you to get through that. You have your husband.

(Phyllis: She was my best friend.)

And you were her best friend and her dad was, too. She adored the both of you. She looked up to you. She was a part of your very fabric. I think there was a side of her that did not want to leave the

roost. (Phyllis: Yes.) She was content. Did she live at home?
(Phyllis: Yes.)

She did not want to leave the roost. How many 25 year olds, the
first thing they want to do is get out of the house? So what does
that say? It wasn't about she had a little comfort zone. It wasn't
about that she couldn't afford to be out on her own. She wanted to
be home. Family was important to her. How many kids do you
know that are like that? (Richie: Nobody!)What a blessing! She was
in no rush to go.

Anymore questions, Rich? Are you good, Phyllis? I am going to end
this in a prayer but I am there for you. God bless you. You are
wonderful spirits. I commend you for what you are doing to help
the masses. You are not taking it all about you. You are taking it out
there. You are exposing it.

(Phyllis: The day that she died, I turned to my son and said "How
are we going to survive this?" because she was really the center of
our family. He said, "We have to honor her every day.) Yes.
(Phyllis: That is what we have been doing.)

When you are ready, and you go up to your vacation place, put your
heads together and come up with a memorial. It could be a bird
bath, anything.

(Phyllis: We started making something already.)

(Richie : Just so we can picture this together. We have 25 acres.
When Dora was a little girl, nine years old, she named an area in the
woods "Dora Lane." It is a path to the stream. She knew. She knew
a lot of stuff for a long time. This weekend was the first time we
went up there since December when she was there with us. She

wanted to spend New Year's Eve there with the whole extended family. Phyllis just started working on her special area this weekend. Changing some rock walls into stone seats. It's beautiful. We are making a meditation garden for her. She loved it up there. She asked me in the late hours of the night before she died; she said "Dad, will you please take me upstate ? I want to go there. It's magical." I said, "You are too weak to go there." Then she asked me to call the EMT's and take her to the hospital and I told her that if we took her to the hospital, she would die in the hospital. I said, "You can stay right here. This is good." We were at home all together. She agreed.)

You know, I am guessing that you may have more paranormal experiences up there since it is relatively quiet. (Richie : very quiet)

~~~~~~~

The audiotape recording ended but unfortunately, we didn't notice. The remaining time together was not recorded. Points we remember:

The medium asked about a shawl. He said it was on a chair and that Dora wanted me to wrap myself in it to feel her embrace. The soft cranberry shawl is kept on a chair in Dora's room. It was so kindly given to her as a gift by Karen L., a very special close friend and co-worker of mine, in case she experienced chills if she were to have chemotherapy. I often wrapped myself in it while writing this book.

When the medium was talking about Dora being home with God, I asked "Then there really is a God?" to which the medium responded that there most definitely is a higher being that is a warm, beautiful, bright light of love and it is all about love.

In reference to the number 605

ANGEL NUMBER 605 - found on an Internet search at http://sacredscribesangelnumbers.blogspot.com/2011/10/angel-number-605.html

Number 605 is a combination of the vibrations of number 6 and number 0, and the attributes of number 5. Number 6 relates to love of home and family and domesticity, service to others and selflessness, responsibility and reliability, providing for the self and others, and nurturing. Number 6 also resonates with personal willpower, independence, initiative, action and overcoming obstacles. Number 0 amplifies and magnifies any number it appears with, and relates to the 'God force' energy and eternity, continuing cycles and flow, and the beginning point. Number 0 resonates with potential and/or choice and is a message to do with developing one's spiritual aspects as it is considered to represent the beginning of a spiritual journey and highlights the uncertainties that may entail. Number 5 resonates with the attributes of making positive life choices and important changes, adaptability and versatility, resourcefulness, motivation and idealism. Number 5 also relates to doing things your own way and learning life lessons through experience.

Angel Number 605 is a message from your angels that the life choices and decisions you have made are bringing about much needed changes in your life. Trust that these changes are bringing about positive opportunities for you to take advantage of, and the angels are supporting, guiding and assisting you through these changes and transitions. Trust your angels and inner-knowing to guide you in the right direction.

Angel Number 605 indicates that the efforts you have made towards changing your life for the better and expressing your spiritual truths have been acknowledged by the angelic and spiritual realms. The angels wish to commend you on your diligence and determination and send you blessings, love and support. You are encouraged to continue making positive changes in your life as they will lead to ongoing personal happiness and success on many levels. Angel Number 605 also suggests that your financial and/or material world is about to undergo some positive changes and you can expect a much welcomed new addition or possessions to enter your life.

The angels encourage you to develop self-awareness, flexibility, resilience and the capacity to reflect upon past mistakes and learn from them.

Chapter Eleven
Number 605 Reappears

We felt such joy whenever we pulled into the driveway of our home and saw Dora's car parked there. She had a bright yellow 2000 VW beetle. The idea of selling her car was almost as painful as seeing it parked there after she passed. I can't even begin to describe the depth of sorrow when it was time to remove her personal things from the car. Everyone recognized that bright, happy looking car as belonging to Dora. She loved it. Everyone did. It brought a smile. Isadora's sister, Tania, drives a 2000 VW beetle as well, only hers is black in color. In May, while Tania was babysitting one afternoon, a neighbor of the family she was working for commented to her on how cute her car was. The neighboring teenager would be getting her driver's license soon and would love to drive a similar car. She asked Tania if she knew of anyone who had a similar car for sale. Tania shared about Dora and mentioned her car.

A few days later, the neighbor and her mom came to our home to see the car and to express condolences. They assured us that they would treat the car with the utmost respect in Dora's honor. In conversation, we asked the neighbor when she would be turning seventeen and receiving her driver's license. She replied, "June 5th." This date is often written as 6/05. It was as if Dora was telling us that it was okay to let go of her car and that this was the person she wanted to have own it now.

Chapter Twelve

The Giving of Gifts

Dora clearly directed me to reach out to her friends on her behalf. I heard her, without spoken words, tell me to enter her room and look in the top right hand drawer of her dresser. There, in the back, I would find a bag holding her Alex & Ani brand bracelets. She received her first one as a gift from her very close friend, Christine. Dora wanted Christine to have the beautiful bracelet back and to keep it as a bond between them. Since I was new at being the receiver of messages, I texted Christine to make sure that I was not making this up in my head. I needed to confirm that it was she who started the Alex & Ani craze at our house and that it was this particular one that was being described to me by Dora that was the original gift from Christine. Of course, it was. My doubt dissolved. Christine was very touched when she received the bracelet back in the mail, knowing it was what Dora wanted. I was amazed and grateful that Dora could direct me to do her bidding so clearly and I began to feel purposeful again for the first time.

A few days after that experience, I was given another very specific direction from Dora. This one involved her sister's closest friend, Mel, whom Dora viewed as a second younger sister. Mel was over the house visiting and as soon as I saw her, I immediately knew what Dora wanted me to do. I excused myself from the room and began searching the house for a very particular jacket that Dora was telling me that she wanted Mel to have. It was black with white piping and very stylish. Mel majored in fashion at college. It took about ten minutes of searching before I said "Dora, you will need to show me where the jacket is. I can't find it." Instantly, I knew where to find the jacket and I went to retrieve it. When I brought it to Mel, and told her that Dora wanted her to have it, she was so surprised, moved, and grateful. When she put it on, we realized it completed her outfit as only Dora, the fashion queen, could have seen. The whole experience was very surreal and magical.

Over the course of that first month of Dora's passing, she continued to guide me in this way.

Chapter Thirteen
Diana's Dream

Sent: Wednesday, May 07, 2014 4:02 PM

Hi Phyllis,

I couldn't wait to email you because last night I had the sweetest dream. Isadora came to visit me in my dreams!!! I was sitting in the back of my car with two other people and Isadora jumped in the driver's seat and started to drive. She was so happy to drive us and kept saying "Let's go, guys!" as she was smiling and in a very good mood. When I woke up, I couldn't believe she was in my dream. I couldn't stop smiling. Although I never had the chance to meet Isadora....that's exactly how I expected her to be ....always smiling!! I believe she came to visit me because I always say a prayer for you and Isadora. I think she was giving me a sign. I just wanted to share this with you. I can't wait to see you in a couple of weeks to walk together as a team to honor sweet Isadora.

I am an elementary school teacher. Diana teaches at the same school. Andrea, yet another teacher, generously organized the rest of the faculty to participate in a Liver Foundation Walk 2014 in Isadora's honor, for which we will always be deeply grateful.

To include Diana into the magic of Dora, I emailed her the transcript of our time with the medium and she sent me this response:

Sent: Friday, May 09, 2014 11:30 AM

My Dearest Phyllis,

What can I say... I'm blown away. Thank you for sharing this with me. This experience validates my beliefs. I truly believe in God, prayer, angels and signs. I so needed to hear this because I too have questioned my own faith. I always ask why do bad things happen to good people? I will never know why but what I do know is that the power of prayer, angels and signs do exist. This also confirms that Dora came to visit me so I can reach out to you! I felt her happy energy!! She was extremely happy!! My dream now makes sense to me. In my dream, Dora jumped into the driver's seat. I believe she was trying to tell me that she is in control and leading the way. I am so honored that she is now my personal angel. :) I am hoping that this experience can bring you some comfort. I can't wait until she visits me again!

Chapter Fourteen

A Facebook Message From Across the World – May 2014

This exchange is as an example of how Isadora's kindness was remembered by someone years later and very far away. Dora positively affected so many lives. Each of us has this potential.

Yashu: May I know with whom I am chatting with? I knew Isadora from high school.

Phyllis: Mom.

Yashu: I knew Izzy when we were in freshman year. She is an absolutely wonderful person in my memories of her.

Phyllis: That is very kind of you to share. She was an extraordinarily kind and selfless person. We miss her every moment of every day and live to honor her memory and continue her goodness. We hope you are well and enjoying the gift of life.

Yashu: I moved back to India after sophomore year…and never got a chance to get in touch with her on FB…I can't believe I missed talking to her…I am truly sorry for your loss…when did we lose her?

Phyllis: March 6th of this year. She had a cancer that only 200 new cases a year are reported. Very rare. No cure. Even the disease she had to get was special. She was very sad because she loved life and helping people. This is why we immediately started a foundation so she could continue helping others even after she passed. She was very brave and fought hard. Her site is isadoraseibert.org. We were so consumed with grief; we created it the first week she had left. We feel her spirit and love all the time though. She had wanted to visit India very much.

Yashu: I wish I could say something to make it better, but I know my words can't help…She will be missed very much. Thank you for sharing…

Phyllis: Thank you for your kindness. I know Dora is smiling now, feeling very touched by you. Be well!

Yashu: Thank you and please take care! Let me know if I can help in anyway…Best regards.

Chapter Fifteen

Forever Family Foundation Weekend Retreat

July 2014 - Chester, Ct.

The Forever Family Foundation (foreverfamilyfoundation.org) was holding its annual retreat, with a special evening set aside just for parents who have lost a child. In attendance were the volunteer organizers and about 18 parents of children who have passed away. Each family had their own tragic story of loss and the medium addressed each family. These are notes and not an exact transcript of what took place when Dora sent her messages to us through medium Laura Lynn Jackson.

Laura Lynn to Richie and Phyllis:

"The moment I saw you, I heard the name "Christine." Who is Christine?" *(Christine is a close friend of our daughter.)*

"Well, Christine is so beautiful. She is honoring your daughter every day with her actions. She is more than a friend. She is family. You need to stay in touch with her always. Keep her close. She is so beautiful and helping your daughter to do her work."

"Your daughter is thankful that there was hospice for her and very thankful for how things were. You cared for her at home, even though it was harder on you both, but it was better for your daughter and she appreciates that. She is thankful for how much you loved and cared for her. You made her feel so good."

"She is saying that she is honored that you are her father."

"There is something about your socks (Richie). You wear socks with your sandals." *(lots of laughter)*

(This was true! When Richie used to wear his Birkenstocks in the winter, he wore them with socks! His children were not amused).

"Richie, she wants you to buy new underwear!" *(lots of laughter)*

"Phyllis, she likes you in the color orange. She says that you are very artistic and that there is so much light and healing energy in you."

"Your daughter is coming through flowers. She is giving you signs through your flowers. They are blooming better than if you used Miracle Gro! That is because of your daughter."

"Don't be afraid to talk to her. You are not bothering her. She says you (mom) are worried that you are bothering her and you are not. She welcomes it."

"Your daughter is very intelligent. Dual majors. Spoke another language."

"She is showing me a white house. It has white shutters and sunlight coming through."

"She is way up in the light. She is very evolved. She has an important job where she is."

"Your daughter is so beautiful. Very kind and loving. Very proper. She knew the deal of what would happen but she chose you as parents. She wanted to come back to let you be her parents. She came just to be loved by you both. You know she is with you."

"Her cancer had spread. She went through three things to try and stop it but there was no chance. She knows you tried everything. Just know that even if she had seen a doctor earlier, it would not have helped. She wants you to stop thinking "Why her? She was so good." She knew the deal. She wants you to know that she is not missing out on anything. Don't feel badly. She came just to be your child."

"All of your kids *(speaking to all the grieving parents present)* are hanging out together today. They brought you all here and they are together now. Your daughter (Dora) is hanging out with their son (points to Angie and Marty). He is a little rowdy. They are going to be putting on a light show together tonight."

"What is with a clay bracelet? She is showing me a bracelet made of clay beads."

"Your son is younger?" *(No, older).* "I thought he was younger because she is telling me that she is always watching over him."

"Your daughter is so beautiful, inside and out. She showed me so much about the two of you. She is not done with humanity yet. She has so much more to give. You are doing so much for her. There is so much more to come. She is going to do so much to help others. You won't believe it! She is not finished yet. So much more is going to happen!"

Examples of how Dora is coming through flowers, as Laura Lynn had stated, that first spring and summer.

A Wisteria plants grows all across an archway by our front door. While it is fast growing and covered in seasonal green leaves, it has never had a flower bloom since it was planted 13 years ago. This is a photo of its first bloom, right underneath Dora's second floor bedroom window after she passed. It has not bloomed again since.

Chapter Sixteen

The Drive Home

The medium had told all the parents to pick something to serve as a sign from their children. She even said to make it difficult because spirits love the challenge. She also made it that we had to ask our loved ones for these signs as spirits will not engage unless requested to do so. On the way home from that event, I thought about what Laura Lynn had said. I chose Dora's sign for me to be a bright yellow Volkswagen Beetle because that was the car she drove. There aren't that many out there, compared to all other cars anyway. Hers was bought used and was now fourteen years old. Within moments of silently expressing this request to Dora, a bright yellow Volkswagen Beetle drove past us. I knew right then that Dora and I would still "talk" with each other.

There have been so many instances since then when, at just the moment I so desperately needed it, a yellow Volkswagen Beetle would appear. My response is always the same: a loud shout of "I LOVE YOU, DORA!" a teary smile, and a feeling of being so loved by her.

Chapter Seventeen
Loving "Hellos"

Dora has visited us in other ways, as well. Frequently, a bird will fly to where we are and fearlessly just sit with one of us. Sometimes, a cardinal will fly across our windshield as we are driving in our car at just the perfect moment. It is very common for people to feel they are being visited by their loved one through the presence of a dragonfly, a butterfly, or a cardinal.

We have continuous cardinal visits, regardless of where we are, since Dora transformed. I like that term better than passed on or even transitioned. She has transformed and even that she has done beautifully. So many of these loving hellos that spirits send to their loved ones tend to have wings. There must be something to that.

A hummingbird and a butterfly visit us in our garden.

Chapter Eighteen

A Sign of Recognition

I was driving by myself on an under populated road in upstate New
York, crying as usual, and talking aloud to Dora. Pleading really.
Asking her to come back, to stay with me, to change everything
back to the way it was. Intellectually, I knew this could not happen
but I had to voice it at that moment anyway. After painful tears, I
asked Dora to show me a sign that she was listening. Since
requesting Dora to use a yellow VW beetle as a sign of recognition
and communication she has. I begged her to send such a car in my
path to let me know that she had heard me. Instantly, a yellow Jeep
from an oncoming ramp pulled in front of me. I said, "No. Not
good enough. Right color. Wrong make." Within a moment or
two, coming from the opposite direction, a silver VW beetle
appeared. I laughed out loud as that is the car that I drive. I knew
then that Dora was with me, showing her sense of humor. I
responded with "Close, but no cigar! Right make. Wrong color."
Within an instant, a yellow VW beetle passed me on the highway. I
was so filled with Dora's love and am so grateful to her that she still
finds ways to be playful and share herself with me. These loving
acknowledgements are not limited to her family either. Many of her
friends have shared with us that Dora is very present in their lives,
as well, using signs that are uniquely perfect to their relationships.

Chapter Nineteen
Past Lives Regression Therapy
July 2014

My connection with Dora made me feel that she was my home. She was my comfort spot. We often did not even feel the need to talk at all when together. It was never forced because our thoughts were as one. I needed to understand why we were so close and more importantly, how I was expected to continue living without her. I came across Barbara Angelo, a past life regression therapist and certified hypnosis instructor (barbangelo.com) who has the gift of helping people find answers to their questions through past life regression. I was with Barbara for over three hours and left feeling comforted. Barbara is a very loving, warm person. Unfortunately, due to technical problems, my session was not recorded. However, Barbara took notes as to what I was saying under hypnosis. Her notes from my hypnosis session are as follows:

First life discussed was in 1817 Massachusetts as "Lisa" who emigrated from England for "freedom."

Lisa had 2 children and in Massachusetts gave birth to a 3rd who died a few months later. It was a boy whom she described as "beautiful." When Lisa died, she was surrounded by her grown children (her husband was pre-deceased). She was considered very old for the time.

At death, she rose up and flapped her wings. She stated she had no arms, only wings covered in white feathers. She recognized others like her with wings that were also moving towards the light. Halfway, she stopped on a cloud to rest while some others moved forward toward the light. They were done with their lives on earth, but "Lisa" said she had to go back to find someone. She was very emotional about this.

We then went back to the first time she knew Dora, and she found herself in the year 503 A.D. and they were twins! They were sitting up on a blanket outside, happily playing together, somewhere between 9 months and a year old. Phyllis's name was "Clare" and Dora was Dora—she was always named Dora in all of her lives. Phyllis was so happy to see Dora. Lots of tears. Lots of tears.

Moving up to 12 years old, they both have long brown hair and Dora is looking at a boy she likes and who likes her. Clare is so happy for her.

In her 20's, Clare (Phyllis) is cooking for her family (husband is the same as in this life - Richie) and Dora lives close by with her own family. In their 30's, Dora is dying. Clare states that she is "old." Clare is with her when she dies saying "I love you- I will always love you." She helps Dora's husband and children and 5 years later she dies as well – from heart issues. When her spirit leaves, she again flies with white wings "always with white wings." God sent Clare (Phyllis) back to earth to share love and to be a "reflection of God." God told Phyllis "change people for the good, then you can come home." Phyllis said "I have to make a difference." God said "Give of yourself. Don't stay alone. Go out there - share my love!" Phyllis said, "Dora's in the light waiting for me – one more time I have to go back."

We then go to another life:

"I am a ruler. A woman ruler who is known for her compassion. I rule to protect everyone."

She is in the desert and Phyllis's name is "Sheba." Palestine. Very long ago…ancient. Dora is not in this life. Tania (her present daughter) is here. She is Phyllis's advisor. She is a male and brilliant. Sheba (Phyllis) "rules thousands of people and protects them from bad rulers and invaders. They need to live in peace." She rules for 19 years, dies from old age – no children. "The people were my children. I was too busy to marry. I loved all the people - they were my family."

Phyllis said she has had 10 lives. She said "I come from God."

68

"Dora's happy – not sick. She's loving and visiting so many on earth – they sense her in different ways – she makes them happy. She changed everybody. She doesn't understand – she's different – she's protected from evil. She's an angel sent here from God a few times."

"I was so lucky to know her - I am grateful."

"Dora was Hilton's sister in another life. I was their mother in Hilton's last life."

"Hilton (her present son) has gifts he has to share – he has to find these gifts. He has to come out of his shell. His gifts are compassion and love; and he can invent things to help people. He's special, too. We have a special family."

"We will be together - the 5 of us again. I just have to wait."

Chapter Twenty
Never Doubt That I Am With You
Summer 2014

We were far away from home, attending an event that Dora would have as well, and deeply drowning in grief. We decided to go for a walk rather than remain crying in our hotel room. Quietly, we exited the hotel property together and walked down the road. We ended up sitting on a bench in a deserted office park. The weight of our sadness was so heavy. The distraction of the walk did not help lighten our burden. We felt defeated and headed back to the hotel. We crossed into a busy parking lot used by numerous stores and restaurants. Shocked, we stopped when, right in front of our feet, a yellow Volkswagen beetle slowly drove by. Immediately, we looked at each other and gasped. The make and model, so similar to Dora's car, shook us out of our sadness. As it continued through the lot, we noticed its license plate and began to cry.

It was a clear message from our beloved Dora that we must feel her presence rather than her absence. As we continued to walk back to the hotel through the lot, yet another yellow Volkswagen beetle passed before us! What are the odds?

We understood why we were pulled to take that walk in the first place. It was not coincidence. Not sure if there is such a thing as coincidence anymore. The timing. That first license plate. The specific car type. The color. Two of them, within a moment of each other.

Chapter Twenty One
I'm with you, Mom
December 2014

The day before the Christmas holiday break was to begin; I drove home in a car filled with gifts my students had so kindly given to me. The radio station played a beautiful a capella choir singing of Christmas. The world was on the verge of celebrating and, even still, I just cried from sadness. There was no celebration in my heart. There was no joy. There was only a desperate longing for my beautiful child. Once home, I sat at the kitchen table, barely listening to Richie give an account of his day. Tears just fell from my eyes on their own volition. I felt numb and the world felt pointless. Richie stopped his story and asked if I heard a bird chirping. He went to the window and opened the shutters. There, at the kitchen window sat a red cardinal, clearly shouting "I'm here, Mom. I'm with you." While the cardinal had moved into our backyard, he never flew to the side of the house making his presence known at the kitchen window before. He had never called to us in such a clear and obvious way at the most perfect time. Dora could not have been any louder unless the cardinal flew in the house and sat on my hand. Even from the dimension in which she exists now, Dora always makes me feel better.

This past October of 2016, while preparing baked goods in the kitchen for her Foundation's Coffee and Dessert Fundraiser, the cardinal returned to the kitchen window. I was feeling so much love for her as I was baking. I viewed this as an opportunity to still do something for her as her mom. I heard the small call of the cardinal and looked up. There, on the closest branch to the window, sat the cardinal 12 inches away looking at me. It felt like Dora was saying thank you to me in a way that I would understand. She still doesn't understand that it is I who is indebted forever to her.

Chapter Twenty Two

Medium Bobby Brust

January 2015

Meeting with psychic medium Bobby Brust reaffirmed that Dora exists somewhere more than just in our hearts and minds. It is so wonderful that certain people have the gift of being able to communicate, translate almost, messages from one dimension to the next. Bobby is very gifted and we are grateful to him. Below is some of the conversation that transpired with Bobby. *(Our responses are in italics.)*

Who is Joe? And who is Anna?

Johanna is Isadora's middle name.

Did you just come back from a trip to Florida?

Yes.

Who is Mickey?

Mickey? I don't know. Oh! Mickey Mouse! Disney World was her favorite place!

I can see that. Is that where you went?

No, but we were nearby and did visit some Disney stores.

Well, she is showing me that she was with you the whole time you were in Florida. Last summer, did you find peace at your place in upstate New York?

I did only when I was working on a meditation garden I am making in her honor. I only feel some peace when I am doing something in her honor because then I feel like I am still her mom.

You will always be her mom. She will always be with you. I see the garden is made from rocks and stones.

Yes.

Did you see a lot of butterflies? That was her. Who is Jessica?

Jessica is her first cousin. (She also has a close friend from her college days named Jessica.)

Well, tell Jessica that Dora says hello. What are all these Japanese things I am seeing?

My parent's home is decorated that way.

Well, tell your parents that Dora says hello to them, too. I'm seeing Native American Indian things. What is that?

I don't know. We have a lot of Asian Indian things but not Native American. Oh, wait. We have two statues at the front gate of our upstate house that are Native Americans.

That's what I am seeing. It is a Native American Family.

Yes! One is a mom holding a baby on her back and the other is the dad.

She doesn't want you to move them.

Wow. We were thinking of putting something else there.

She sees that her closet is the same. Her room is the same. Have you changed anything?

No.

She is recognizing that. Who goes in her room and talks to her?

I do. I sleep in there sometimes to feel closer. Richie goes in and talks to her, too. Her room serves as the center for her foundation as well.

Well, she hears everything you are saying. She knows you are there. She will always be with you. She is never leaving. She made it to the other side but she will always be with you.

So, you found the sewing machine?

Oh my God! I did! (Dora and I had wanted to start sewing clothes before her diagnosis. After she passed, I thought I should find the machine and try sewing anyway to honor her. I didn't know where the sewing machine was for years and I had just found it!)

What's this about a deli? Or food business?

Don't know. Richie's dad was a butcher.

Okay, that explains it. I saw meat so I thought of a deli. Well, she is with your dad, Richie.

Did she know him?

No. He died when I was nine.

Well, she knows him now!

Richie then asked: *Do you see light? What color light are you seeing pertaining to Dora?*

I see dark blue and purple.*

She is very present at the place upstate. She is very present at the NJ house, too. She will never leave you.

(According to the book Journey of Souls, *by Michael Newton, Ph.D., which Richie was reading at the time we had this session, the highest soul color is purple, next is dark blue, light blue, dark yellow, solid yellow, yellowish-red, and white.)*

Chapter Twenty Three
Transcript with Medium Doreen Molloy
September 2015
(Our responses are in italics.)

Nine months had passed and for us, it was enough time to feel that we needed to revisit a medium and hear from Dora through words. I contacted Doreen via her website. (doreenmolloy.com) She is also very gifted, professional, and compassionate. Here is a transcript of the helpful meeting Richie and I had with her.

Let me just open your circle right now and let's just see who is around. You guys have a lot of energy on the other side. Wow. I'm actually just going to start as I am scanning above you as I feel there is a lot of older energy around. There is a very strong mom figure here. Did one of you lose your mother? Both your moms are here? She wants to identify as the mom figure. She is giving off a mom vibration. I don't know who she is yet. It could be somebody who is very close to you that lost their mother, it could be an in-law. There is a strong mom energy around her and there is an M connected to her somewhere or with her name. You have several older female figures though. There are two males above you that come together, who are above you, who are connected or are really close. They could be brothers but they are above you so that is going to be older generation. There is a male off to your side and a male above you. They are connected. When I say to your side, it is someone of your generation. Did one of your friends lose a son or a nephew?

There are several young energies with little life experience. There is also a younger female on the other side beneath you. Is this your daughter? Is this who you were most hoping to hear from today? I know I will hear from her today. I was feeling a younger energy even before you got here.

Wow! She is a strong energy. She has not been gone long. This is a recent passing. Was it this year? Has she passed recently? (*a year and a half ago*) She's been around you. She is giving you a heads up that you know it is her without a doubt. She says you have felt other people, too but you know when it is her. You can tell the difference between her and other energies. I feel that there is so much tragedy around her passing. I feel like you got the rug pulled out from under you because of the way this happened. She talks really fast. I have to get her to slow down! Her energy is so speeded up! (laughter) She is showing me a lot of symbols and that there were a lot of questions. She makes me feel that some of the questions might have been answered but some were not. She goes like this (snaps her fingers). She crossed over like that. May I ask was your daughter not at home when she passed? She is telling me something about being out or having gone somewhere. I am not sure of the significance of that but she is mentioning it. I'm feeling a lot of chaos and confusion. Things were in an upheaval or things were not going the right way. (*She thought she would live*) It's just a lot of chaotic thought that I'm getting. Was there an article written about her? (*Yes, in the high school newspaper where she taught.*) Because she is saying "Wow!" She is showing me that they put her up on a pedestal. Do you have a garage in your house? Is there something in the garage? She is telling me to tell you about the garage. Was there an incident or something in there? Did you feel her when you went in the garage? (*A cardinal came to live in the bushes next to the garage after she passed.*) Many people tell me about cardinals. She is telling me to mention that area so there is something of significance she wants you to see. (*As of the writing of this book, two cardinals, a female and a male, live there now.*)

The cardinal in the bushes near the garage.

She says you have a book with her writing in it. She knows that you have it and that you look at it. Do you have another child in addition to her? She is saying she isn't the only one. She makes me feel that she wants me to acknowledge one of them for an achievement. Did one of them graduate? Was there a graduation? (*Yes. Her sister graduated from college.*) She wasn't here for it but she knows about it and she saw it. She wants you guys to know she is around you a lot.

She says to tell you she sits with you in the kitchen. "I am in there with you." (*She liked to cook. We liked to cook together.*) She is referring to a pasta dish right now that you make that no one else makes like that. (laughter)

I know how terribly traumatic this was for you, her passing, but she wants me to mention it was not traumatic to her. You're here one minute and then gone. It's very important that you know this but not to worry. Boom! She just went. She had an inner knowing that this was going to happen. My sense of her is that she knew she wasn't going to be here for a long time. She wasn't going to grow old and that she tried to pack as much as she could into her life. This is a very vibrant soul! I want to get as much as I can out of my time here and I'm going to do everything! You know what she just said to me? "I am like a whirling dervish!" and she is laughing! She is confirming this for me.

She says you are still in touch with her friends (*Yes.*) She is so happy about that. They talk to you. They call you. They come to see you. (*I wanted to make her happy about that.*) She is and that is why she is bringing it up. She knows that a lot of people miss her. It's not just you guys. Her friends do, too.

She says I'm supposed to talk about the music or the band. Did someone dedicate playing music for her? Can you tell me about this? (*She stayed connected with her first nursery school friends, her elementary, middle, and high school friends, her college friends and in the past few years, she socialized with her co-workers. When she made a friend, she stayed friends with them for life. After she passed, there was an American Cancer Society Relay for Life event and it was at her college alumni school. Many of her college friends came back to the school and participated in her honor. A group of them are musicians. Her friends had a photo of her up on a giant screen and her friends played music at the event. It was so humbling.*)

She is giving me goose bumps again! Your daughter has so much gratitude for everyone who has honored her, who was a friend to her, and to you guys. She is making me feel like she knows what you are going through. They always do, and she doesn't want you to feel that sadness forever. But, we miss them so there is no easy way. She makes me feel that you guys are the best. You were always there for her (*The three of us were very close.*)

May I ask you, was she in her twenties? She wants me to share something with you. She says that there are children around her on the other side and I get that she is very drawn to children. These are children that passed and she is making me feel that she is the meet and greet. Do you understand? She is fulfilling something that she couldn't finish (*When Dora was told that she had cancer in the terminal stage, she cried, "Oh my God, I'm not going to be a mom!" Maybe she is getting to feel like a mom now.*) She has a nurturing energy. Not all souls show me those kinds of things. They don't always show me an activity or a particular thing like that on the other side because the afterlife is not a place. The afterlife is a frequency. A lot of people think it is a place, like it is somewhere we go but not really. This is why people like me can sense your loved ones around you. It was like a light bulb moment for me because they are actually in the same time/space that we are in. That is why they are always around us. They are still right here. Your daughter is still right here. Her energy is still right here. The afterlife is not a place.

Occasionally, they will show me something that was so meaningful for them that they feel that they have to complete something, or participate in something on the other side because it is cool or because it was important to them in some way. It will come out in different ways.

I see lyrics or poetry. Who is the person that writes, that writes poetry? (*Our other daughter.*) She is putting her hands on her heart like "wow," that is so cool whatever she writes. She says she is good at it! Your daughter is so vibrant (*She certainly was.*) No, she still is! You have to understand something. It's the same energy! Her energy is exactly the same as when she was here. Her personality traits, her memories, all her bonds of love that she made here for people, it's all intact.

May I ask you is this an odd form of cancer or unusual (*Yes, very rare.*) because she is showing me that this was not run of the mill. They don't know what to do with this. They don't know how to treat this. But, I am also feeling this is systemic. In other words, it was not localized in one area. (*It was a form of liver cancer. When she finally had some symptoms and we went to a doctor, it had metastasized.*) Yes, she is showing me that now. (*Only 200 new cases in the world every year.*) That is pretty rare.

I like her energy so much. She is so vibrant. (*She is so likeable.*) Let me tell you, your daughter is telling me she really has a lot of friends. She is making me see that for her service, when she passed, she was like "holy cow!" I don't know if it was standing room only or people couldn't get in, but there was a line. (*Over 1000 people came.*) That's incredible! She is making me feel like (*I'm so glad she knows about it!*) Yes, she does. (*Good.*) They usually attend their own services. (*Really?*) She really makes me feel like "Wow! Wow!" because so many people loved her.

Is something on a plaque somewhere too? Up on a wall? (*Yes. There have been plaques placed all over the place!*) She is making me feel that it was not just at her passing but that she is memorialized in other places. (*Yes.*) She is very honored by that.

I meant to tell you something. There is a really strong intuitive side with her because I feel like she just had a real way with… what is that expression when someone is a good judge of character and they can size someone up just like that? (snaps fingers) She is very intuitive, almost border-line psychic when she was here. She knows stuff. She doesn't know how she knows it but she just knows stuff. She had a feel for that kind of thing.

This is a sister who writes the poems? (*Yes.*) Somebody has her jacket she said or her sweatshirt or something you wear over your clothes. Who has this? (*I do!*) She is glad. She says you can feel her when you put this on. Just know that whenever you put this on, she is giving you a hug. That is her hug. (*Okay.*)

Do you guys have a dog? (*Yes.*) She says that dog knows when she is around. Dogs, and cats too, can sense energy. You can see your dog looking around and there is nothing there but it is wagging its tail. She is saying that the dog has felt her. (*He goes in her room and lies down on her bed.*) The dog senses her energy and that is not your imagination. She is around you guys a lot. Let me say something for a second. It is very hard for our loved ones on the other side to interact with the physical world. In other words, it takes a lot of energy for them to do that. It takes some kind of physical interaction with the energy here so that we can sense them around.

She is telling me that she has given you guys some signs (*Yes, she has.*) Just know how determined she has to be because it takes a lot of energy for her to do that. She is letting you know "I'm right here! I'm right here!" She is jumping up and down right in front of you. She plays with things. She plays with things inside the house.

This was not a hard passing for her. I need to emphasize that. Everything just kind of stopped and she says she just went to sleep. Very, very fast her passing. Not hard. Literally. She is with one of her great grandmothers on the other side. I know our great grandparents pass before our kids are born but she is making me feel that she has some kind of connection to one of them. (*Her name*). Is that your grandmother, Phyllis? (*Yes. Dora. She was named for her. Also, I called that grandmother "Mom." Her nickname was Mom.*) This must be who I mentioned before when I was talking about a mom figure. She is with her.

She lost a friend, your daughter. It was either someone she went to school with, or college with, that passed away. I do feel that it is female and she passed before your daughter did. She passed a few years ago. She is over there with her. Also, there is an uncle. Did one of you lose a brother or brother-in-law? (*I lost my uncle a couple of months before she went*). Okay, because I am feeling that he is there. She is there with family but there are other people there also.

She just told me that there is a dog also on the other side. Did you guys have a dog that passed? (*Yes. Bowtie*). She says "I have the dog. Don't worry." I just heard the dog bark! (laughter) Our pets get to be with us. A comforting thought for any of us who are animal lovers. (*Will we get to be with her?*) Yes. Yes. Why do you think she is telling me who is there? Because we all stay together. (*Okay.*) The circle of energy is anybody who has a connection to each other. It is not always just family. Friendships are going to be in our circle. Animals are going to be in our circle.

Did you have family that liked to grow tomatoes and herbs? I am seeing like a farm and rows of plants. (*I do that.*) Okay, was that taught to you by parents or grandparents? She has people around her on the other side that liked to do farming. Elders. You grow tomatoes don't you? She just told me that. "It's tomatoes! Tomatoes!" She says you are good at it and you like to grow things. I don't know where this comes in but there is a horse there. Maybe from one of your families a few generations back but she wants me to tell you that there is a horse there. I don't know which side it is. You have to ask your extended family about this to validate it. (*Richie: My grandfather had a horse.*) There you go because she says the horse is here, too. She threw that in because she knew I was saying to you that we can have extended family members, friends, etc. and so she says the horse is here by the way. (*She is so cute!*)

Do you wear her picture? Do you wear a locket? (*I wear her name necklace.*) Do you have a locket with her photo or you know how people have an ID thing on a chain? (*I keep her driver's license with me.*) That's it! I was almost going to say it was something laminated or something with her image on it. Okay, so she knows that you have that. You take her with you wherever you go even without her image she says. You never need to have that to talk to her; just talk to her all the time (*I do.*) She says she hears you, she hears you, okay? You feel her in the car (*Richie: I do*) all the time (*Richie: all the time*). She has really given you signs all over the place. She is literally nudging you "I'm here!" so just know this. This is the thing I can't emphasize enough. It is not your imagination when you are feeling her. It is not! It is not wishful thinking. This is what a lot of people think that, "Oh it's just me. I'm missing her." But no, she is around you.

Now you said you had a reading with another medium. She said she came through that reading like gang busters. Your daughter's energy is very clear and she is a really good communicator. (*She was a teacher. She drove a bright yellow* bug.) That shows you the personality that she has! That is very reflective of that. (*Another medium told us to pick something as a sign and even make it a difficult one. They like the challenge. So, I picked her car because it was just so her. Ever since then, just at the perfect time, a yellow VW bug will go by.*) There is interaction there, very clear interaction. She has worked above and beyond the call of duty to make sure you know she is hanging out with you guys and that even though she can't be here physically, she is with you. Her spirit is very bright, very vibrant, and very connected to you.

She just told me that there is an event over the next year or so, something happy, a celebration, so you may not know about this yet but the family will come together. This gathering, she will be there. She wants to make sure you know she is attending in spirit. She has such a fun personality! (*Richie: She brought the fun.*) Yes, she did. She says don't forget my sense of humor. (laughter) She would make people laugh. And not always intentionally! (laughter)

She says never worry that she is alone. She says there are many people with her. Some she wasn't here on earth with. Maybe they passed before she was born and she didn't have a relationship with but she is making me feel that there are so many here she never feels alone.

She is a very deep thinker your daughter, very much so. She just said she was ahead of her time. She could really project or like an old soul where things she would say you might expect out of an eighty year old but she would say it. You would be like "wow!" Where does that kind of wisdom that comes from age come from? But, that's just who she was. That is part of her personality.

She lived home with you guys? (*Yes.*) And you kept some things intact? She is telling me something is still intact (*Everything.*) and things are still where she placed them. Her things are still there and she says you feel her very strongly in there. (*I'm not touching anything.*) She will never leave you. She will never leave you. Her spirit will never leave you. Listen to me, if you redo that room, or one day you decide to move, or whatever the case is, you carry her in your heart. She says "You feel me no matter where you are."

After her passing, did you start buying books about life after death? She knows you are reading them because she knows that you have to know that she is okay. This is her chance to tell you that she is and very much connected to both of you. I feel like when she is with you, when she is around you, she is very playful. Her energy is very light and playful. It is almost like she will nudge you in such a way that you will want to smile, even though I know grief is a very hard thing. She just showed me that she came to you in a dream. (*Yes.*) She says "That's me! I can come to you in a dream!" (*She is such a good girl.*) (laughter)

Do you have connections where we are right here? In Hudson County? (*One of her closest friends, Christine, lives here in Union City.*) Because she just said there is another connection right here.

After her passing, you said it was March of last year 2014, was there something you canceled? Because she just said "I want you to go on vacation." (*We did, eventually, take that trip.*) I want you to do that. (*We canceled the original trip, which was planned for the Fall of 2014, because Dora was part of that reservation. We all had hoped she would be going.*) She wants you to have fun. She wants you to go on vacation again. She says it is good for you to be out and to do stuff. (*She is so giving.*)

I don't know if you noticed but during this whole session she is talking a lot about people that are here. She isn't talking about people who passed or about herself. She wants to talk about everyone who is here, about you guys, about what she sees is going on. That is where her focus must be. (*So family minded.*) Well, you guys have a really close family. She is showing me that. She has her arms around every body and is pulling everyone close together. She has a very big energy your daughter. Very intense. Very alive. Very vibrant. Remember whatever energy she was here, she is there. We don't have a spirit, we **are** a spirit. We have a body. (*Richie: A day before she passed, she said she didn't want to be in this body anymore. Phyllis: She recognized that she was not her body.*) She differentiated by saying that to you guys. This is just a vehicle. This is just the vehicle we use to travel through this earth school. We need the body to travel through this earth field. But it doesn't define who we are. It's our conscientiousness that defines who we are.

I love that your daughter is so vibrant because she is able to show me that she did collect a lot of experience for her years, even though she couldn't stay very long. I see it that we come into our physical life with a soul contract and the contract just sort of represents what we come here for, what we want to learn. Part of the contract also includes who we are going to share this experience with; our family, our friendships, we come into our soul group. That is why people have soul mates. That's why people have karmic connections because there is soul recognition when you come together. (*I had that with her.*) I always tell people a soul mate doesn't have to be someone you marry. It can be a sibling, a close friend, it can come in anyway. Your daughter is showing me that you two laughed a lot. You were buddies. (*Best friends.*) It's not just mother-daughter, which was also close, but you were buddies and she says "I loved hanging out with you." We decide what we are going to work on here with our soul contract and we also choose, not on a conscious level, when we are going to depart. If we were conscience, that's all we would think about and we would never get into the business of living. But, what happens when we check off all the things that we wanted to do here, it's okay to go. There is a bigger spiritual picture when it comes to our journey here.

She says you have a million questions to ask. She is telling me that you are always searching for the deeper answers. (*Well, I am always sad because I miss her so much.*) Yes, that is the hard part (*But, I am happy that she is okay.*) She is okay. She is okay. She is with others. She is surrounded by children. Your daughter loves children and she is good with them. She makes me feel like that is just where she wants to be and as children crossover, she is right there for them. That is her way of fulfilling something that was very important and deep to her. She couldn't do it here but she can do it there. (*My oldest, my son, is married. They don't have children yet. It upset Dora that she wasn't going to be here to be an aunt to their kids.*) Well, here is the other thing. They see us and hear us. They are all around us. She will watch as children come into the family. They are kind of seeing and taking part from spirit in that environment I guess you could call it. She will see the family grow.

So, you don't have any grandchildren? (*No.*) She says that there is a boy coming. A boy is coming. Not yet, she says, but a boy is coming! She says, "Hold your horses because the boy is coming!" She gets to meet him first before he gets here. She is making me feel like a boy is coming and that there will be two kids. She is showing me two fingers so I feel like there will be two from your son and daughter-in-law. She has very protective energy around all of you.

She is telling me to tell you (to Richie) to take care of something you have been ignoring, like go get something fixed or check out (*A physical thing?*) Yes, it's not something big but she wants you to feel good. (*Richie: Thank you, Dora.*) It is something you haven't kept up with. She is being your reminder. You have something in the house that has her name on it – a cup or something like that, she says. (*We have a mug with one of her signed drawings that she made in art class at school when she was ten years old. We also have lots of coffee mugs that say Isadora J. Seibert Foundation from its annual coffee fundraising event.*)

She is a very loving energy, your daughter, she never held back on that, a very giving spirit. She would put everyone ahead of herself, very giving. That was the way she was and that's the way she wanted to be and the way she still is. It's more about everybody else. She is just a beautiful spirit. So many people loved her. (*Yes. She taught everybody how to be kind.*) Yes and that is a monumental skill that is priceless. That kind of thing was important to her. (*Richie: It was everything. Phyllis: She taught through example.*) Yes. Okay, did she ever share with you, I'm not getting all the information but this just flashed in front of me, she was a teacher? She taught younger kids? (*High school.*) Was there a young boy, maybe a freshman that had some kind of major issue or problem, where she actually stepped out of the role of teacher and helped him out? (*Yes.*) Because I feel her say, "I step out of that role and do something extra on a personal basis." That's who she was. That's a very giving soul because it wasn't about this is my job and this is my paycheck (*Oh, no.*). She loved all these kids. Everybody that she came into contact with, a relationship developed and she truly cared about everyone. She cared about them.

I have to tell you also that physically she says her energy was so drained that it was okay for me to go. That the last ditch effort wasn't going to work and that it was okay for me to cross because I was tired and I couldn't sustain any quality of life anymore. It was okay and she is okay on the other side. I don't know if I have to tell you this or not but the minute we make our transition we are whole and complete. Just think about it. We are not dealing with anything we had to deal with here on earth because that is all connected with our physical bodies, injury illness, whatever. It is pure energy. Pure spirit doesn't have to deal with that anymore so she is whole and complete. On some level, I feel that her transition was very freeing for her because her body wasn't working anymore. It's like being trapped in that body that wasn't working so when she said she didn't want to be in her body anymore, she meant it. She understood, even at that point, I know there is going to be something else for me. I know I am going to be okay. I can't do this anymore. I think it was so hard for her to stay in that body. She is showing me pain issues and she is not dealing with that anymore At the same time that you are sad and grieving that she can't be here anymore, celebrate that she is free of that body that couldn't work anymore.

She will continue to give you signs and signals to let you know that she is around and it will be comforting for you. It will be. She is saying remember all those silly things she said. (*If we remember her with joy and with love but without the sadness, will she still know how much we miss her?*) Oh, yes. That is something that never goes away. That bond can never be broken. Ever. The bond is never broken. Just because you guys are still here physically and she can't be here in physical form doesn't mean the bond isn't perfectly intact just like when she was physically here. Don't feel like you are dishonoring by fully living. (*I do feel like that.*) Don't feel like how can I be laughing if she is not here? Believe me when I tell you, trust me in this, they want you to feel joy in your life again. They want you to be able to breathe again and just kind of let go of the pain. They can see us. They know what grief is like. Do you think she wants you to be hurting and suffering when she is right here with you?

I hope this helped you today. (*Tremendously.*) She is not alone. There are a lot of people there. Family stays together. Friends that you bond with stay together, too. Whatever you are doing, keep doing because you feel your daughter so strongly. I don't know if you two feel her at the same time. I am getting that she likes to interact with you separately. It is easier for her to interact with you this way and give you each undivided attention. Love is forever. Never forget that. There is nothing that is going to break that bond. Love is forever.

Hey, are you (Richie) having trouble with your knee? (*Yes! Today I am! I had trouble coming up your stairs!*) She just showed me that. She wants to know if you are having trouble. She just asked what happened to your knee. (*Richie: I really feel her.*) We communicate with them through telepathy. There are no secrets. You think it. She hears it. Soul to soul. This is why mediums do this to show that consciousness survives physical death. I hope this helped you guys today. She is helping you from over there, she is your teacher, on how to connect with her because she is trying so hard to communicate with you. You will continue to get communications with her because she knows it makes you happy.

Chapter Twenty Four

A Paper Cardinal Still Counts

Toward the end of the 2015-16 school year, I began to reorganize things in my classroom in preparation for the start of the upcoming fall school year. I went into the attic storage space of the school where I teach to find some items I had previously placed there. It was dark and hot but well organized with everyone's supplies. I knew where my things were so I crawled into that corner beneath the pitched roof. I couldn't stand up in that area. I came across my life size poster of William Shakespeare and immediately thought that it would be perfect for my daughter Tania's classroom as she is now a high school English teacher. I smiled at the thought and crawled back out. As I stood up, I saw something at my feet that definitely was not there when I first entered the storage space.

It was a child's coloring of a red cardinal. I knew instantly that it was a sign from Dora that she was agreeing that the poster of

Shakespeare would be wonderful for her sister. I don't know why this paper cardinal was in the storage area as only teachers' possessions are kept there, certainly not student work. I don't know how it suddenly appeared as I turned to leave. I just know I felt Dora communicating with me yet again. I felt her loving her sister, loving me, and continuing to be an active part of our family.

Chapter Twenty Five

Continuing Messages of Love

We have almost endless stories to share about signs from Isadora because she has continued to make her presence known and it is now three years since she transformed. We have included only a few of our first experiences in this book. But, they all tell us the same message:

"I love you. I am still with you. I am okay."

Nevertheless, the enemy, our own thoughts, can still come in and cause so much sadness. Dora is probably saying to us, "What more do I have to do to get my message across to you?" I hope she continues her messages, albeit with less frustration, because the exchange of love that is felt is beyond description. Dora can still impart such joy. We can still share love. Always. Even though we exist in different forms now. Nothing is stronger than love.

Cardinals live in our yard now.

Epilogue

First and foremost, *truly* love the people that you do, in fact, love. By this I mean, try to love unconditionally. It isn't easy unless you have someone like Isadora in your life. If you don't, then *be* someone like Isadora. It works both ways. It is a challenge for most of us, most definitely for myself, but it provides a goal or a purpose to life. That true exchange of love may be the key to receiving signs from someone who has transformed. Honestly, I have no idea how it all works. Grief is an experience none of us are exempt from. I can only humbly suggest that you share yourself with others. We all have so much love to give. At the very least, be a kind person. When someone you love first transforms, or even if their transformation was years ago, ask them for signs and then *pay close attention* for those signs. Some may be obvious while others may be subtle. You will know in your heart when you are being sent their love. It is very palpable. At first, you may feel like the signs are coincidences. But, after awhile, it will become clear to your broken heart that so many coincidences are just not possible. Be open to the love being sent to you. It is the only thing that has kept me alive. I will forever love and adore you, Isadora Johanna Seibert.

Isadora was a victim of fibrolamellar hepatocellular carcinoma; a very rare form of liver cancer found mostly in teens and young adults who are healthy in every other way.
Symptoms usually do not appear until the disease is well advanced. A liver resection is currently the best chance at treatment but there is no cure at this time. Very little is known about this cancer. By the time Isadora exhibited symptoms and was diagnosed, the cancer had metastasized. She was twenty-five years old.Isadora exhibited tremendous grace, bravery, and love throughout her ordeal.

We are very grateful to each person who thought of her, prayed for her, gifted her or our family with some form of physical support and/ or emotional support, and to those who are able to financially support her foundation. We send our love to all those who have been affected by the epidemic of any form of cancer.
Thank you all.

To find out more about Isadora, please visit isadoraseibert.org and Isadora J. Seibert Foundation on Facebook.

Remember to shine your light, especially in the face of darkness.

FightFibrolamellar is a campaign to support fibrolamellar research at Rockefeller University, where the chimera that causes this disease was first discovered.

The Fibrolamellar Registry offers a searchable forum, organized by topic.

Fibrolamellars of the World Unite! is a closed Facebook group whose members have been affected by FHC. There is tremendous support here. To become a member, send an email with your request.

The Fibrolamellar Cancer Foundation funds selected research projects on fibrolamellar and sponsors a yearly patient gathering in Vermont. The FCF was founded by Tucker Davis after being diagnosed in 2008 with FHC. He has since passed but the foundation continues.

The Max Burdette Fibrolamellar Cancer Research Foundation is trying to raise funds to start a fibrolamellar research clinic at St. Jude's Children's Hospital.

The Cancer Survivors Network, part of the American Cancer Society, has a fibrolamellar-specific discussion page.

Isadora J. Seibert Foundation

isadoraseibert.org

Made in the USA
Middletown, DE
12 November 2023

42538231R00060